FOURTH DOWN AND LIFE TO GO

HOW TO TURN LIFE'S SETBACKS INTO TRIUMPHS

SEAN COVEY

FOURTH DOWN AND LIFE TO GO

HOW TO TURN LIFE'S SETBACKS INTO TRIUMPHS

Bookcraft
Salt Lake City, Utah

Library of Congress Catalog Card Number: 90-83212

ISBN 0-88494-772-6

2nd Printing, 1990

Printed in the United States of America

To Rebecca

who has made my life
a journey into light

CONTENTS

Foreword ix

Preface. xiii

1   The Lord's Success Formula   1

2   Ask Not for Victory But for Courage   11

3   Why Don't You Just Eat More?   25

4   Missions, Dominoes, and Dirty Little Kids   39

5   My Worst Birthday Ever   51

6   Me a Quarterback?   63

7   The Spiritual Creation   73

8   From Starter to Backup   81

     Epilogue   87

FOREWORD

Sean Covey represents everything that is good about athletics. He has known the highs that can come from winning a championship game and the lows of being injured and losing a starting position that was his for two years. And more important, he has learned how to handle both with courage and integrity.

I first knew Sean as a stocky little boy who lived around the corner from our house. As I would drive home from work each day, I would pass his house, and the park just across the street. Invariably he would be playing football or some other game. This was not unusual in and of itself; many young people spend hours playing one game or another, but Sean was one who had an intensity about everything he did. He always worked very hard to be the best, whatever the task. And Sean excelled not only on the playing field but also in his academic pursuits, which he attacked with the same intensity, graduating from college with a 3.8 GPA and with University Honors, BYU's highest graduation distinction.

What is it that motivates the Sean Coveys of this world? If we knew, I'm sure we could bottle it and sell it for large sums of money. After thirty-eight years of coaching at both high school and college levels, I know from experience that those young athletes who go on to excel have the ability to see within themselves what they truly can become. Self-visualization is such an important trait to have. It can be learned or developed by each one of us if we will but take the time to figure out in our own minds what it is we would like to accomplish. We must then develop a plan of action. What is it I need to do? Set up a logical step-by-step process that will help me reach the intended goal. Know where I can go for help, whether it be to a coach, a teacher, a spiritual leader, a book, or all of the above. Then, finally, just simply go to work. Hard work is the catalyst that will bring it all together.

It is interesting to ponder on all the time and effort required from a football player in order to play eleven or twelve times in an entire year. During January, February, and March there's weight training and conditioning, maybe three hours a day, four or five days a week. Then there is spring practice followed by more weight training and conditioning during the summer, then fall camp, and of course all the practicing, coaching, traveling and playing during the regular season. Playing major college football requires a year-round commitment combined with Spartan-like self-discipline—all for eleven or twelve games. The players who can't visualize their greater potential simply cannot muster the discipline necessary to be successful.

When a player is trying his hardest, striving for perfection, giving everything he's got, he's experiencing a lot more stress, a lot more pain, than the player who is merely going through the motions. I remember a statement by Don Scholander, a great swimmer. In talking about swimming he remarked that where the threshold of pain turns into agony is where champions are born. Those who can stand the agony will finish the race.

There are many unknowledgeable football ''fans'' who think the coaches and players just show up on a Saturday in the fall and decide to play a football game. Those who know, realize that it takes a lot more to win a game, let alone a championship. Coaches and players alike have to use this self-visualization; they have to know what they want to accomplish that year. There are many planning meetings, teaching meetings, and scouting meetings that take place before the team ever hits the field for practice. Goals are set, plans are made, and the work begins. This is true in football and it is true in every aspect of life.

In the field of athletics, we tend to look at successful athletes and make them almost bigger than life. I have seen many young men who have achieved greatness. I have also seen those who have come up a little short of their potential. Every year on the BYU football team there are players who are bigger, stronger, and faster than those who are playing in their position. Why is this? I'm not sure, but after so many years of coaching, one overriding principle stands out: Potential does not always ensure success. In other words, the greatest players have not always been the most endowed. In athletics, we often hear the phrase, "He has the will to win." I think this is wrong. We can be in a game, taking a test, giving a talk, or whatever the experience may be. We can have the greatest will to do well. But unless we have prepared, it is of little use. Really, it should be the "will to prepare." Those who succeed have this will, whether it be in athletics, in school, in their chosen vocation, on a mission, or in almost any other phase of their life.

Those who succeed have also the ability to overcome adversity, disappointment, and even tragedy in their lives. How well do we handle adversity? Adversity is going to be with us in everything we do, almost in every facet of our lives—in our personal associations, in the mission field, in our chosen professions, in our families. When we have adversity we oftentimes tend to look around and think that we're the Lone Ranger. We tend to believe that we're the only one who has problems. And we always look around and see others who are more talented, taller, smarter, handsomer, or faster. I can assure you, everyone has problems—even football coaches. The ability we have to handle this adversity will determine the degree of success we will have in life. To me, this is where the gospel can be the greatest of help to us.

Sean truly represents all of the above. He was not a "gifted" athlete, but he was a young man who had potential and the "will to prepare." He knew it would take a tremendous amount of commitment on his part to reach his goals; that is, to be the best quarterback he could be, to be the BYU starting quarterback, and to lead BYU to a championship. He did become the starting quarterback at BYU and, through his striving to be the best, he led them to two consecutive bowl games, the 1987 All-American Bowl and the 1988 Freedom Bowl.

Aside from all of his achievements on the field, there is one experience with Sean that will always be with me. It happened during the fall of the 1989 football season. After starting for most of the 1987 season and all of the 1988 season, at the conclusion of the latter season Sean sustained a knee injury requiring major surgery. This meant that he was not able to go through spring practice leading into the 1989 season. A young man by the name of Ty Detmer had a tremendous spring and fall camp and, as a result, Sean lost his starting position to Ty. When I called Sean into the office, I explained to him our decision to go with Ty. Although very disappointed and hurt, he looked me in the eye and said, "Coach, I'm sorry about the decision, but I just want you to know one thing. I will be ready if you ever need me." And he was a man of his word. Sean never missed a practice or a meeting and was totally ready emotionally, physically, and mentally to play each week; never complaining, completely supportive of Ty and the program. This is what Sean is all about. A total team player.

Sean has captured the essence of these principles and many others in this memorable book. His philosophy, experiences, and examples provide thought-provoking and compelling reading. I would truly recommend *Fourth Down and Life to Go* to people of all ages, especially to the youth who are making choices now that will have great significance later in their lives.

R. LaVell Edwards

PREFACE

This book is about football. And about life. The fourth down situations. The critical moments of life. And about how to get first downs.

This book is about the best of times and the worst of times. It is about triumph. And setback. And about how to turn setbacks into triumphs.

This book is about private battles and painful windsprints. It is about girlfriends and great friends, moms and dads, missions and marriages. In short, this book deals with all the ordinary events and challenges of daily living.

Playing football, both as a starter and a backup, has taught me some valuable insights about life. For instance, football has taught me that God is personally involved in the nitty-gritty details of our daily lives. And that being strong in the hard moments can make all the difference. Football has taught me the necessity of building our foundation upon that which is unchanging. Football has taught me where the power comes from to see the race to its end. And that power is not in football. It is found deep within each of us and within gospel teachings.

I wrote this book for young people and for everyone who deals with young people—parents, leaders, teachers, and coaches. This book would also provide valuable help for anyone who needs additional watts of courage. Anyone whose emotional life resembles a roller coaster. Or anyone who desires to draw up new blueprints for his or her life.

I am deeply grateful to the following people who have shaped my life for the better, and to those who have helped in the creation of this book:

To Mom and Dad, the two most influential people in my life, for teaching me that life is a mission and not a career; and for their example, which demonstrates that living the gospel and having a whole lot of fun go hand in hand.

To my brothers and sisters and their spouses for their affirmations of me, for their good lives, and for their continual readings of rough drafts.

To Richard Bouchard, my best missionary companion and a great friend, for his example of living the abundant life. Richard truly loved life, loved people, and was loved in return.

To Frank Henderson, my high school football coach, for providing four years of memorable times and for truly believing in me.

To LaVell Edwards for his friendship and for his shining example of levelheadedness.

To all my good friends for their loyalty and for their exertion of positive peer pressure.

To Cory Maxwell, George Bickerstaff, Jana Erickson, and the other fine people at Bookcraft for their professionalism and for providing me with such a positive experience my first time around.

1

THE LORD'S
SUCCESS FORMULA

*Search diligently, pray always,
and be believing, and all things
shall work together for your good.*
—D&C 90:24

"What's wrong with you? Where's the Sean Covey I once knew in high school?" My quarterback coach glared at me in disgust. "Do you even want to be out there?"

I was shocked. "Yes, of course," I stammered.

"Well, to me you look like you're just going through the motions and your heart's not in the game. And if you're not careful"—he spoke gravely—"the younger quarterbacks are going to pass you up and you're never going to play here."

It was my sophomore year at BYU, during the middle of another hot, fall football camp. I knew something was amiss when coach asked me to meet him in the football office after practice. But I had no idea his words would be so jolting.

Eighteen months before this confrontation I had returned home from my mission in South Africa with a dream and a challenge before me. The dream: to become the starting quarterback for BYU. The challenge: to get my now-flabby body back in shape. I set a goal to become the starter in my sophomore year.

Another goal was to become an all-American. Weights, passing drills, and whole-wheat spaghetti became my daily routine. Every ounce of my 170-pound frame thirsted for that starting position, or so I thought at the time.

Four of us were competing for the top job that year. Imagine my embarrassment when I learned at the close of spring camp that I was fourth string on the depth chart. The coaches also decided to redshirt me, which meant I could practice but couldn't play in the games. That's like dating a girl for over a year and never even getting a single kiss. Still I continued my intense four-hour-a-day workout sessions in preparation for my sophomore season. I was determined to secure that starting position somehow.

I thought I had been playing well in my sophomore year—that is, until this confrontation. Coach's accusation that I was just going through the motions deeply affected me, not because he bawled me out, and not because he was disappointed in me, but because deep down in my heart—down below all the hard work I prided myself in doing, down below everything I said about wanting to become the starting quarterback—I knew he was right. It hit me like a revelation: even though I was killing myself physically, somehow I had not completely given my heart and mind to the goal. And the discipline of the heart and mind is a much higher discipline than that of the body.

At home that night I sprawled out upon our hard kitchen table, against Mom's wishes, rehearsing his pointed words: "If you're not careful you're never going to play here." How true those words rang! I realized that without a wholehearted and resolute commitment I would never play. Over the next few days I measured my internal reserves to see if I had sufficient resolve to make that kind of commitment. I also considered quitting. After all, in addition to full-time schoolwork, football would take thousands of hours over the next three years, and unless I was truly committed, body and soul, it wasn't worth my time.

"The real tragedy," said President Kimball quoting Arnold Bennett, "is the tragedy of the man who never in his life braces

2

himself for his one supreme effort—he never stretches to his full capacity, never stands up to his full stature" (*The Miracle of Forgiveness* [Salt Lake City: Bookcraft, 1969], p. 94). I've never enjoyed tragedy. So I welcomed President Kimball's challenge and decided to brace myself for a three-year-long supreme effort.

To rise to this higher level of commitment I knew I would need a new strategic game plan that would draw upon the powers of heaven. I don't believe our Heavenly Father cares about football itself, yet I do know that he is interested in our character growth, and if football can provide that, then the Lord is interested in football. This kind of connection may have been part of what the Lord meant when he said, "All things unto me are spiritual" (D&C 29:34).

Over the next several days I found and developed my game plan. I drew the philosophy of it from a scripture found in D&C 90:24. It might be bold of me, but I call this scripture the Lord's success formula. It reads, "Search diligently, pray always, and be believing, and all things shall work together for your good." In this scripture the Lord promises all of us that if we will search diligently (which to me means work hard), pray consistently, and believe, all things—including football or whatever our interest might be—will work together for our good.

It seemed simple. All I had to do was work, pray, and believe, and the Lord would take care of everything else. Did this mean that if I did my part the Lord would make me the starter? Of course not. The Lord cares just as much for other quarterbacks as he does for me. The promise says that all things will work together for my good. Maybe it was for my good to become the starting quarterback, or maybe it was for my good to be a bench warmer. I didn't know. But I did know that the Lord knew, and I had faith that if I did my part, he would do his—he would magnify my football abilities.

So I began working, praying, and believing. I began setting specific goals, not monthly or weekly, but practice by practice. After practice I lifted weights, ran sprints, threw balls, and watched game films. I tried to develop a friendship with my

3

horselike, 275-pound offensive lineman. In short, I did all I could to *work* diligently. At the same time I made a sincere effort to develop and maintain a closer relationship with my Heavenly Father through *prayer* and to involve him thoroughly in my game plan.

Most important, I *believed*. For me this was the hard part; but this was also the key. This was what I had been lacking before. As Joseph Smith taught, believing or exercising faith requires mental exertion, mental sweat; it requires the discipline of the heart and the mind. I had to learn to put my faith in the Lord's way of doing things and in the Lord's formula for success rather than in my way of thinking and in my way to success.

My game plan began paying immediate dividends. By the end of fall camp I became the sole owner of second string.

The 1987 season began. Games passed one by one—Pittsburgh, Texas—and I saw no action. My arm hung limp after these games because I had warmed up all game long. After all, "What if I got in?"

At times I was struck with the discouraging realization that, despite all my effort, I might never play quarterback for BYU, as our starter still had another year. That frightened me, especially considering the hundreds of hours I was sacrificing for football. But I recognized that worrying about things outside of my control was faithless. I was using my way of thinking, my arm of flesh. So each time I felt discouraged, each time I found myself worrying about how well the other quarterbacks were playing or what the coaches were thinking, I exerted myself mentally and exercised faith in the Lord's way of thinking: work, pray, believe, and focus on that which you can control—yourself. And when I did this I felt at peace.

Ever so slowly, I kept improving. Things which once seemed impossible for me became easy. Let me illustrate specifically. I have a small hand and never had confidence throwing a fully inflated football. This was no problem in high school because I threw deflated footballs. But in college everyone uses fat, fully inflated balls. Moreover, college refs inflate the balls to the size of watermelons. After returning from my mission I decided to throw a narrower brand of football in practice, different from the lardo brand the varsity used.

But the facts were plain: if I wanted to start, I would have to throw the fatter ball. At the start of fall camp, to my mind effectively throwing that watermelon was absolutely, positively, and in all other ways inconceivable. So I specifically involved the Lord in this problem and set daily goals to conquer it. I put my faith in his way of thinking, not mine. His way states, "All things are possible to him that believeth" (Mark 9:23). In a matter of weeks I was throwing that melon ball better than I had ever thrown a deflated one. To me these results were miraculous. It felt as if I had just won the Heisman Trophy.

In the third game of the season we played the Horned Frogs of Texas Christian on their home field. Early in the game, as in the days of the Mormon pioneers, the sky began raining crickets, blanketing the artificial turf. This proved to be a sign of things to come—our team was being devoured. Since we were so far behind, I sensed that tonight might be the big night, my first chance to play. And like a flock of sea gulls I would save the day.

Sure enough, in the third quarter my call came. "Covey," Coach Edwards summoned. "Warm up." I took a big gulp. My heart pounded. My head swam. "This is it!" I thought. "After all these years." I paced up and down the sidelines, envisioning the newspaper headlines the following day—"Covey, in His First Game, Leads Cougars to Comeback Victory."

It didn't turn out that way. We lost the game badly, although I did squish a lot of crickets. I didn't play too poorly, but I didn't set the field on fire either. I was just plain average. And to earn a starting job my playing had to be outstanding, not average. In other words, I felt I got my chance and blew it. After the game it was said that my arm was too weak to ever make it in college football. It was a long plane ride home.

The games continued to roll by—New Mexico, Utah State, Hawaii—and I continued to see little or no action. "Remember the game plan," I told myself. As each game approached I made it my rule to prepare myself as if I were the starter even though I was just a backup. I kept working, praying, and especially believing. And I kept improving. The coaches took notice.

Midseason featured the big game of the year. We played the Air Force Academy, on national television, in Cougar Stadium, in front of sixty-five thousand fans. At the time, Air Force was nationally ranked. And they paraded the best defensive tackle in the nation: a 260-pound, one-man, bench-press-a-million, quarterback-wrecking machine.

The Monday before the big game my quarterback coach (the same one who had confronted me earlier in the season) called me into his office. By his peculiar manner and tone of voice I knew something was up. "Sean," he said, eyeing me across his desk, "You're our starter for Saturday's game. And you know how badly we need this one." My heart skipped a beat. And as his words sank in, I felt my inner resources convert from six to eight cylinders. To succeed, I would need that additional horsepower. That night, in secret prayer, I thanked my Heavenly Father.

Never have I been as focused on one thing as I was that week. I must have seemed totally spaced out because I didn't hear people when they spoke to me. My mind was elsewhere. It was Beat Air Force or Bust.

Game day was rainy and cold. Before going to eat pregame breakfast with the team, I pulled my warm comforter around my shoulders, glancing at the rain-soaked terrain outside my window. "Seven hours from now we will be victors or defeatees; I will be a hero or a bum," I thought. The anxiety was awful. Yet deep inside, because I had religiously followed my game plan, I felt prepared and at peace.

The game arrived at last.

At kick off my mouth was so dry I could barely talk. And after one quarter of play, before we knew what had happened, Air Force had scored twice while we had garnered minus 6 yards total offense and zero first downs. Though being double teamed, Mr. Defensive Tackle had spent more time in our backfield than I had. Unless we could generate some offense very quickly, the game was lost.

In these circumstances I recall standing on the sidelines, fighting off the doubts which tried to creep in: "This is much more difficult than I ever imagined." "If I don't hurry and lead the team to a score I'm going to get benched and I'll never play again." But I'd prepared myself for tough moments such as this. I prayed silently, exercised faith in my game plan and in all my preparation, and told my mind to clam up!

From that point on I began to lose all concept of self. The Lord helped me forget that I was playing on national television and in front of sixty-five thousand fans. I even forgot about the defensive tackle machine. I just felt like a little boy playing a fun game of football out in the yard. And things began to click.

We beat Air Force that day 24–13, and somehow I was even named the ESPN player of the game. I had achieved my dream of becoming the starting quarterback and was able to maintain that position for the remainder of that year, and for all of the following year.

After the game my eight-year-old brother said to Dad, "I'm sure glad we won the game."

"Why's that, Joshua?"

"Because now they won't call Sean a bum."

Going from backup to starter proved to be a valuable experience, not because I became the starter but because I discovered the Lord's formula for success in D&C 90:24. I discovered again, as I had so many times before, that the Lord is personally involved in the nitty-gritty details of my life. Even though football is only a game, he cares about football because it is important to football players. And most important, I discovered that if I will work, pray, and believe in the Lord's way of thinking, I can live with confidence and without worry, knowing that all things are working together for my good.

The Lord didn't hand me the starting position. But he did magnify my football abilities far beyond what I thought possible. And thus, when the opportunity arose, I was prepared. I will ever be grateful to my quarterback coach, Norm Chow, for seeing through my mediocrity and jump starting my better self.

The Apostles of Christ had various day-to-day needs and

worries. Apparently they asked the Lord, or were thinking: What shall we drink? What shall we wear? Where shall we sleep? And Jesus answered by saying: "Your heavenly Father knoweth that ye have need of all these things. But seek ye first the kingdom of God . . . and all these things shall be added unto you." (Matthew 6:31, 33.)

In like manner, we have daily needs, and worries, and questions: Am I good enough to try out for the baseball team, the debate team, the school play? How can I get this boy or girl to notice me? What should I major in? How can I overcome this weakness of mine? What can I do to become accepted, popular, even successful? Or my question: How can I become a better quarterback? If we remove ourselves from these questions and view them from afar they may seem insignificant, even trivial; but when we own them, when they are ours, they become very important and very real. The Lord recognizes this. He knows that such things are important to us, and he has provided the answer as to how to obtain them.

The answer is always the same: put God first by living his gospel and applying his success formula, and he will magnify you in all that in righteousness is important to you, whatever it may be. This he has promised. He will help you in your athletic endeavors, in your relationships, in your schoolwork, and in all your tough decisions. He will help you overcome seemingly insurmountable mental blocks, your personal, fully inflated footballs. His help may not always be what you want at the time or what your "arm of flesh" thinks is best for you, but it will be what the Lord knows is best for you. And isn't it exhilarating to know that all things are working together for your good!

One of my favorite movies is *Chariots of Fire*, the true account of the 1924 British Olympic track team. I am especially inspired by the shining example of the Scotsman, Eric Liddell. His words reveal his belief that God is involved in all of our extracurricular activities. "I believe God made me for a purpose, but he also made me fast. And when I run I feel his pleasure."

Eric Liddell also believed in the Old Testament verse that reads, "Them that honour me I will honour" (1 Samuel 2:30).

You see, Eric recognized that his power to run came from God, and that if he would honor God by keeping his commandments, God would honor him by making him fast.

His belief was put to the test in the 1924 Olympic games held in France. Eric learned that his event, the 100 meters, was scheduled on a Sunday. And for Eric, to run on the Sabbath was to break it. He could not defy his conscience. Instead he entered as an underdog in the 400-meter race with a firm belief that if he honored God, God would honor him. *History of the Olympic Games* records the outcome as follows:

> Undoubtedly the dark-horse of the 1924 games went to E. H. Liddell, a bandy-legged little Scotch divinity student who, driven from his favorite event, the 100 meters, by his religious scruples, which prevented him from running on Sunday, surprised himself and everybody else by winning the 400 meters in record time.
>
> Liddell, an awkward runner who obviously was unfamiliar with the distance, set out like a scared jack rabbit at the sound of the gun and fought off the challenge of H. M. Fitch of the United States down the stretch to cover the distance in $47^3/_5$ seconds.

God has also made all of us for a purpose, and when we develop our various talents we will feel his pleasure. We honor him by living his gospel and by applying his success formula to our lives; he honors us by magnifying our talents and by working all things together for our good.

I know that when I strive to live the gospel through offering my prayers, reading the scriptures, and serving others, I become a better football player, do better in school, develop higher quality friendships, and so on. I think we too often emphasize the idea that "good guys" never prosper and that they must wait until the next life to receive their reward. Too seldom we emphasize Nephi's words, "He that is righteous is favored of God" (1 Nephi 17:35) or King Benjamin's words stating that if we obey God's commandments "he doth *immediately* bless [us]" (Mosiah 2:24, italics added).

There might be others, many others, who seem to have great talents without even being religious at all. Many win awards and are paid big bucks and they actually belittle those who follow God. But they will never know true peace and their ultimate potential. They will never know true and eternal success without the Lord's formula. And as President Ezra Taft Benson put it, the formula pays better:

Men and women who turn their lives over to God will find out that he can make a lot more out of their lives than they can. He will deepen their joys, expand their vision, quicken their minds, strengthen their muscles, lift their spirits, multiply their blessings, increase their opportunities, comfort their souls, raise up friends, and pour out peace. Whoever will lose his life to God will find he has eternal life. ("Jesus Christ, Gifts and Expectations," *New Era*, May 1975, p. 20.)

2

ASK NOT FOR VICTORY BUT FOR COURAGE

Physical courage, which despises all
danger, will make a man brave in one way;
and moral courage, which despises all opinion,
will make a man brave in another . . .
but to constitute a great man both are necessary.
—Colton, The New Dictionary of Thoughts

As a young boy I lived for the Dallas Cowboys, and my older brother Stephen worshipped the Minnesota Vikings. We knew everything there was to know about our teams. We knew all the players' names, their heights and weights, and even some of their birthdays.

Each week Stephen and I skipped to the mailbox for our prized magazines, *The Dallas Cowboy Weekly* and *The Viking Report*. Our walls were plastered with pictures of our heroes: Roger Staubach and Fran Tarkenton, Bob Lily and Alan Page. Stephen was always a great brother to me—that is, except when Dallas played Minnesota.

During these games we would sit on opposite sides of the couch, and since Stephen was older and bigger than I, I wasn't allowed to cheer. In fact, if Dallas did something good and I showed any sign of glee, Stephen would threaten to pound my face in.

I recall one game in which Dallas beat Minnesota in the final seconds on a long bomb from Roger Staubach to Drew Pearson. Stephen glared at me with fire in his eyes and said, "I know you're happy."

"No I'm not; I'm not happy at all," I replied. What I really wanted to say was, "You're darn right I'm happy. In fact, I don't know when I've ever felt this good!" But I simply said, "I'm not happy."

"You are too," roared Stephen. And with that he pounced on me, slugged me in the head, and then ran into his room, slamming the door behind him.

This is how strongly we felt about our football teams!

Stephen went on to become an outstanding Little League quarterback. On the other hand, football, or competitive athletics in general, was never easy for me. Don't get me wrong. I loved to play neighborhood pick-up games, where it didn't really matter how well you played and where nobody was watching. But I hated to compete in formal activities, where there were officials and fans and where it mattered how well you played. Even in elementary school, I became frightened by the thoughts of being timed in the 50-yard dash or of running against all my friends on field day.

The Provo City tackle football league began when I went to junior high school. Deep down I wanted to play, but I was afraid to. Nonetheless, since my brother Stephen and many of my friends were playing, I felt I had to play as well. It was play or be a wimp. And no seventh grader wants to be a wimp.

When I reported to practice the first day I was a nervous wreck. I had planned to be a running back, a respectable position, but since I was a chubby kid Coach Baldser thought I looked more like a lineman and made me play offensive center, of all things. "Offensive center? What will Stephen say?" I gulped.

After practice we all lined up for what Coach Baldser called windsprints. Sounded like fun to me. Little did I know the level of pain I was about to experience. Suddenly, coach blew his whistle, and we had to sprint to the other end of the practice

12

field. We took off running. Then, before I could catch my breath, he blew the whistle again and we had to sprint back to him. He kept blowing that idiotic whistle until my lungs burned and my legs throbbed. "Surely he won't make us do another one," I thought. And again I heard the high-pitched screech of the whistle in the summer heat. I was positive I would never live to finish my seventh-grade year.

That first practice was one of the most jolting experiences of my life. The thought of having to go to practice the next day, and then the next, made me feel so on edge that I decided to quit.

Deciding to quit was easy. Admitting to my friends that I was going to quit after just one practice wasn't easy. In fact, it seemed as bad as the sprints. The next day at school when my buddy Clar Hofheins asked me why I wasn't coming to practice, I shrugged, "Hey Clar, I wish I could play, but my dad said that if I got hurt, he'd be really mad at me, and I have a feelin' I'm gonna' get hurt, so I better not. Aren't dads a pain?"

The following year in eighth grade I again decided to play football, although it made me uneasy. That year I stuck it out and finished the season. Along with the sprints, I had a few moments of excitement. In fact, I was one of the best players on the team. But overall, I still hated it.

I remember waking up early Saturday mornings and wishing so badly I could stay home and watch cartoons, or wishing I could get sick so I wouldn't have to play. I seldom told my friends or family about our games because I didn't want them to come. After all, "What if I have a bad game?" I longed for the season to end and I was the happiest eighth grader in the school on the day it did.

Looking back I realize it came down to this: I was scared to compete and scared to try and scared to fail. I wanted to kick back and relax in my comfort zone.

Now, what's all this about a comfort zone? I'm coming to that. We all have certain clothes we like to wear, friends we like to hang out with, and hobbies or activities we like to do. These and all other comfortable, risk-free things fall within the circle of our comfort zones. These things are easy for us to do and, like

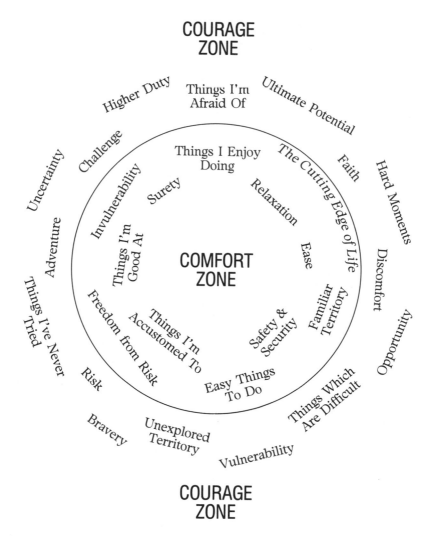

COURAGE
ZONE

Higher Duty • Things I'm Afraid Of • Ultimate Potential • Faith • Hard Moments • Discomfort • Opportunity • Things Which Are Difficult • Vulnerability • Unexplored Territory • Bravery • Risk • Things I've Never Tried • Adventure • Uncertainty • Challenge

Things I Enjoy Doing • The Cutting Edge of Life • Relaxation • Ease • Familiar Territory • Safety & Security • Easy Things To Do • Things I'm Accustomed To • Freedom from Risk • Things I'm Good At • Invulnerability • Surety

COMFORT
ZONE

COURAGE
ZONE

The more we jump into our courage zone, the faster our comfort zone boundary will expand, until things which were once difficult and discomforting for us become easier and more enjoyable. As Emerson put it: "That which we persist in doing becomes easier for us to do; not that the nature of the thing itself is changed, but that our power to do is increased."

old shoes, we're used to them. Within such well-known boundaries we feel safe and secure. (See the accompanying diagram.)

Then again, making new friends, speaking in church, or undertaking anything for the very first time can make our hair stand on end. Welcome to the courage zone! Adventure, challenge, and risk included. Everything that makes us feel uncomfortable lies in our courage zone. In this territory awaits uncertainty. We're not so sure we can come out on top. But remember, the courage zone is also where rapid growth and our true potential are located.

As a seventh grader, tackle football was about three miles outside my comfort zone, since I didn't know how to take a hand off or make a tackle, let alone play center. This was new turf, risky turf. I wasn't sure I could succeed.

On the other hand, eating was definitely inside my comfort zone. It was easy for me, and I was confident I could do it well. My jello-belly was proof of that.

"But what's so wrong about enjoying your comfort zone?" I've often asked.

Nothing. In fact, much of our time should be spent there. But there is something absolutely wrong with *always* staying in that comfort zone. Remember, earth life itself was a huge leap out of the most comfortable of comfort zones for each one of us.

"But who wants to take on risky experiences and painful challenges when you could be emotionally warm and cozy? I mean, we all like to be sure about things, don't we?"

Sure we do. But I also believe that people who never exercise courage and who never attempt because they fear failure, become like old bread and drug addicts, stale and comfortably numb. They experience little strain but little growth, few disappointments but few satisfactions, few setbacks but few triumphs. The risk of riskless living is the greatest risk of all.

By definition, exercising courage and parachuting into unfamiliar territory will make us feel uncomfortable. But let's not worry about that because as soon as we accept the fact that growth is painful by its very nature, it ceases to become pain and becomes something else altogether.

15

The longer I live the more I believe that the key to growing and reaching our potential is to jump outside of our comfort zone on a regular basis. This demands *courage*.

When I was younger I believed that being courageous or fearless meant that I would never feel fear. I was wrong. Being courageous means that you act in the face of fear. When I faded back to pass against the University of Hawaii and five grizzly, 260-pound Tongans wanted to tear my arms out, don't you think I was scared? You bet! But I chose to act in the face of that fear. After a while you get used to that kind of thing. Former BYU all-American quarterback Steve Young would get so nervous before each game that he'd throw up and pray that the stadium would blow up. If there were no difficulty and no fear, there would be no need for courage.

The two thousand stripling warriors spoken of in the Book of Mormon are prime examples of acting in the face of fear. They were all young men, maybe high school seniors, who took up arms to defend their country against the bloodthirsty Lamanites. Their leader, Helaman, hoped to avoid having them fight. But, ultimately, a time came when the young warriors were needed, and Helaman asked them, "Therefore what say ye, my sons, will ye go against them to battle?"

And even though they were all very young and had never fought before, and even though the thought of fighting probably threw them miles outside of their comfort zones, they said, "Father . . . our God is with us, and he will not suffer that we should fall; then let us go forth."

"Never," said Helaman, "had I seen so great courage, nay, not amongst all the Nephites." (Alma 56:44–46.)

We will meet daily with will-you-go-to-battle moments. To speak our loyalty for a friend while others are badmouthing her requires an act of courage. To be honest when it would be profitable not to requires an act of courage. To confront a friend, say "No!" and sometimes say "Yes!" all require acts of courage. Each of these qualities—loyalty, honesty, friendship, "won't" power, and willpower—at their highest testing points require acts of courage.

The great thing about the courage zone idea is this: The more we jump into our courage zone, the faster our comfort zone boundary will expand, until things which were once difficult and discomforting become easier and more enjoyable.

Okay, so leaping out of my comfort zone might be good for me. So are going to bed early and getting up early, but that doesn't get me to do them. What now? To motivate myself to jump outside of my comfort zone I set up goals in my courage zone. That forces me to reach and stretch. I also rehearse three powerful thoughts over and over in my mind.

Thought no. 1: Never Let Your Fears Make Your Decisions

What if, because of their fears, Columbus hadn't sought for a new route to the Indies, Abraham Lincoln hadn't tried to free the slaves, or Joseph Smith hadn't prayed in the Sacred Grove? What if Benjamin Franklin hadn't flown his kite or Nephi hadn't returned to Jerusalem for the brass plates?

When I think about all I failed to do in my life because my fears told me "No," "Can't do," "Don't try," I ache inside. In high school, for years I had a crush on a blond named Sherry. I thought about asking her out for a date but never did because my fears screamed, "Maybe she won't like you." There were classes I never took, people I never sought out, teams I never played for, and goals I never set — all because of these stupid, yet very real, fears. I like how Shakespeare put it:

> Our doubts are traitors,
> And make us lose the good we oft might win,
> By fearing to attempt.

Exercising courage requires faith; it requires us to believe not only in the unseen God but also in the unseen potential within each of us. I believe that the Lord will occasionally manipulate events which will force us into our courage zones — in order to

17

try our courage and faith (see Mosiah 23:21). He understands our fears but, like a wise coach or captain, he still expects us to act in spite of them and is displeased when we don't. "But with some I am not well pleased, for . . . they hide the talent which I have given unto them, because of the fear of man. Wo unto such, for mine anger is kindled against them." (D&C 60:2.)

Of course, the Lord can't always promise us victory; he can, however, promise to fill us with courage, if we will but ask. During my senior year at BYU I was short a few credits, and so I skimmed through the class schedule looking for something to fill the hours. When I came across "Private Voice Instruction," as in singing lessons, I thought, "Now that's something I'd like to try." It was definitely outside of my comfort zone.

One of the reasons why I took private lessons instead of group lessons was that my voice wasn't (and still isn't) too hot. I didn't want to make a fool of myself by singing in front of a group. I figured it would be much easier to make a fool of myself in front of only one instructor.

Things went fine until my singing professor, Houston Hill, brought the traumatic news. "By the way, Sean," he said, "you will have to sing in front of the other private voice students before the end of the semester."

"What do you mean?" I asked in horror.

"Well, the class requirements state that you have to sing at least one time in front of the other students, for practice."

"You're crazy," I said doggedly. "I could never do that."

"Oh, it's no big deal. You'll do fine."

Well, to me it was a very, very big deal. The thought of singing in front of a group made me tremble. "How am I going to get out of this one?" I thought. But I wouldn't allow myself to do that because I was learning to never let my fears make my decisions. For several years I'd been speaking at firesides and advising young people to act in the face of fear. Well—it looked as if I was up at bat.

"Courage, Sean," I kept rehearsing in my mind. "You've got to at least try."

The dreaded day arrived. I walked into that "room of doom" and, to my excitement, there were only about twelve students there. I was expecting twice that. "Hey," I tried to convince myself, "this won't be bad at all."

I soon became intimidated again when I discovered that nearly everyone in the room was either a music major or a theater major. I mean, these people really knew how to sing. Their versions of the classics sounded better than the originals to me. They'd performed in plays, and musicals, and choruses. For them, singing in a crowd must have been about as difficult as conversing with Mom.

My turn arrived and I stood in front of the class, three million miles outside of my comfort zone, repeating to myself, "Courage—I can't believe I'm doing this—Courage—I can't believe I'm doing this."

"I will be singing 'On the Street Where You Live' from *My Fair Lady*," I quivered.

When the piano started playing and all eyes fell upon me, I couldn't believe I had actually gotten myself into that situation. And everyone was actually going to take my singing seriously.

I began singing. I immediately noticed that the expressions of the other students changed from enjoyment to pity; they felt for me. My body felt as tight as Levi's just pulled from the dryer. I had to squeeze every word out of my chest.

Near the end of the song is a really high note. It had always been difficult for me to reach, even in practice. Now I anticipated it with horror. But as that note approached I thought, "What the heck. Go for it!"

I don't recall if I hit that note or missed it. All I remember is that a couple students were so embarrassed for me that they could no longer look at me but had to stare at the ground.

I finished and sat down quickly. I now had to endure their many, well-meaning lies.

"That was great, Sean."

"Thanks a lot," I returned. What else could I say?

But do you know what? Although that experience scared the

19

shoulder pads off me, when I left that classroom and walked out to my car I was so proud of myself. I felt a great sense of personal accomplishment, and I frankly didn't care what anyone else thought about my high note. I had blown it and I was proud of it!

President David O. McKay stated, "The greatest battles of life are fought daily within the silent chambers of one's own soul." And in this private battle the victory was mine.

So the next time you want to
    make a new friend,
        resist peer pressure,
            break an old habit,
                develop a new skill,
                    try out for an athletic team,
                audition for a school play,
            ask out a blond,
        serve a mission,
      speak in church,
    be yourself,
or even if you want to wear something outrageous that may not be in style—do it, even when all your fears and doubts tell you "No," "Can't do," "Don't try." Never let your fears make your decisions. You make them.

"Okay. So I ignore my fears and take action. But what if I fail?" Good question. This brings us to our second thought.

Thought no. 2: Winning Is Nothing More Than This—That You Rise Each Time You Fall

We've heard this so often and it sounds so corny. But it remains so true. Often we are so scared of failing, so scared of being laughed at and ridiculed, that we never try. Read what Harry J. Gray has to say about this:

You've failed many times, although you may not remember. You fell down the first time you tried to walk. You almost drowned the first time you tried to swim. Did you hit the ball the first time you swung the bat? Heavy hitters, the ones who hit the most home runs, also strike out a lot. Babe Ruth struck out 1,330 times, but he also hit 714 home runs. R. H. Macy failed seven times before his store in New York caught on. English novelist John Creasey received 753 rejection slips before he published 564 books. See! Don't worry about failure. Worry about the chances you miss when you don't even try. (As quoted in Dan Clark, comp., *Getting High* [Sunrise Publishing, 1983], p. 82.)

I have always had little respect for the guy or gal who sits back in his or her comfort zone and laughs at the mistakes of the risk takers. On the other hand, I have great respect for the courage zoners of life. Get inspired by Theodore Roosevelt's words:

In the battle of life, it is not the critic who counts, not the man who points out how the strong man stumbled or how the doer of the deed could have done better; the credit belongs to the man who is actually in the arena; whose face is marred by dust and sweat and blood; who strives valiantly; who errs and comes short again and again because there is no effort without error and shortcomings; who does actually strive to do the deeds; who knows the great enthusiasms and the great devotions, and spends himself in a worthy cause; who, at the best, knows in the end the triumph of high achievement; and who, at the worst, if he fails, at least fails while daring greatly; so that his place shall never be with those timid souls who have tasted neither victory nor defeat. (*Getting High*, p. 85.)

My favorite lines from the movie *Rocky* come when Apollo Creed's trainer warns Apollo about scheduling a rematch with Rocky, saying, "I saw you beat that man like I've never seen you beat a man before, *and the man kept coming back.*"

Here are some statistics from the life history of another man who took a beating and kept coming back. This man failed in business at age 31, was defeated for legislature at age 32, again failed in business at age 34, had to cope with the death of his sweetheart at age 35, suffered a nervous breakdown at age 36, was defeated for speaker at age 38, was defeated for congressional nomination at age 43, was elected to Congress at age 46, lost renomination for Congress at age 48, was defeated for Senate at age 55, was defeated for United States vice-president at age 56, and was defeated for Senate at age 58.

This person was none other than Abraham Lincoln, elected president of the United States at age 60. He rose each time he fell, and eventually he gained the respect and admiration of all nations and peoples.

And what about the chicken guy known as Colonel Sanders? His little restaurant was doing fine until the highway which passed by it was rerouted along with the rerouting of his customers. It wasn't much later that he received his first Social Security check. He had to do something. His first idea was to try to sell his chicken recipe to restaurants, hoping to gain a percentage of their profits. He traveled all around the country looking for people to buy his recipe, sleeping in his car. He kept changing his approach and was rejected 1,009 times before someone finally took a chance on his recipe. Today, Kentucky Fried Chicken boasts restaurants worldwide.

If we truly believed that success was found in attempting, in trying, in rising each time we fell, wouldn't that change our entire outlook on life? Wouldn't we be much more willing to try, to risk a little? Wouldn't success be totally within our control?

Thought no. 3: Be Strong in the Hard Moments

My third thought comes from Stephen R. Covey's book *Spiritual Roots of Human Relations* (Salt Lake City: Deseret Book, 1970).

The poet Robert Frost wrote:

Two roads diverged in a wood, and I—
I took the road less traveled by,
And that has made all the difference.

I have come to believe what my dad always taught me: There
are certain hard moments, diverging-road moments, that, if we
are strong in them, will make "all the difference" down the
road of life.

As Christ suffered in Gethsemane and later on Golgotha, he
was baffled, awestruck, by the weight of the combined iniquity
of mankind. It was much worse than even he had ever imagined.
"If it be possible," he pleaded with the Father, "let this cup
pass." All of mankind's hopes, all of his possibilities, even all
eternity hung on the outcome of that moment. "Nevertheless,"
concluded Christ, "not my will, but thine be done." By being
strong in his hard moment and partaking of that most bitter of
cups, Christ made all things possible: eternal life and the eternal
family, repentance and growth, happiness, and every other
good thing. That made all the difference.

Hard moments are conflicts between what we should do (the
straight, narrow, and often stony path) and what would be the
easier thing to do (the elevator or escalator).

Our hard moments may come wrapped in a career choice, a
mission choice, or a marriage choice. A choice between remaining in school or painting for bread too soon. When temptation
strikes, our hard moments may come in the form of controlling
our tongue, our thoughts, or our appetite. Our hard moments
might include getting up on time, resisting peer pressure, or
being honest.

Because they lie within our courage zones, each hard moment will cause discomfort. You and I must be courageous. Are
we also willing to partake of our bitter cups?

John's hard moment arrived each night at bedtime. One side
of him wanted to offer a meaningful prayer, not just another
"Thanks for everything, Amen." The other side felt the big,
warm arms of the mattress reach up and pull him in. Each night,
John was strong in his hard moment. That made all the differ-

ence. Years have passed and John is now enjoying a rich relationship with Heavenly Father, instead of an otherwise shallow and superficial one.

Jessica, when tempted to compromise her chastity by degrees, was strong in her hard moment. That made all the difference. She is now preparing to meet her eternal mate and begin an eternal family, instead of coping with guilt or even an undesired pregnancy.

Eric's hard moment arrived during the week-long finals of each school semester. He wanted to have his cake and eat it too. He wanted good grades and good times. Since final exams would largely determine his grades, Eric knew it was critical to study hard now and play later. On the other hand, his roommates were out swimming, going to movies, and having a grand time. Besides, he felt so beat up by the semester's load that he deserved a break. Eric was strong in his hard moment. That made all the difference. His excellent grades landed him the job he desired and propelled him into a highly rewarding career.

Look around. People who are strong in their hard moments make the greatest contributions to this world of ours.

Let's not fret over hard moments, for they don't come too often. They only come a few times in each person's day; a few times in each person's lifetime. Between hard moments we must store up reservoirs of strength and courage so that when they strike we can stand firm.

Today or tomorrow, in public or private, the opportunity to exercise courage will come. Your fears will cry out one thing, and your better self will communicate another. You alone will recognize the crossroads. Which voice will you listen to?

Be a courage-zoner!

Be strong in the hard moments!

Make all the difference!

Go ahead and fail up a storm as did Abraham Lincoln and thousands of other great men and women, for if you simply rise each time you fall, you are a winner in anyone's book.

In the words of the Prophet Joseph Smith, "Courage, brethren [and sisters]; and on, on to the victory!" (D&C 128:22.)

3

WHY DON'T YOU JUST EAT MORE?

Good timber does not grow in ease;
The stronger wind, the stronger trees.
— Douglas Malloch

"Come on now. Pick it up. You're gettin' fat in the head!" Coach's words bellowed in the summer furnace as we dashed up and down the simmering football field. I glanced to see if my shoes were on fire. "Suck it up! Dig down deep and suck it up! How bad do you really want it? How bad?"

The yammering of my barrel-chested, high school football coach still echoes loudly in my memory. "How bad do you want it? How bad?" It all reminds me of an often-repeated poem:

> If you want a thing bad enough
> To go out and fight for it,
> Work day and night for it,
> Give up your time and your peace and your sleep for it:
> If only desire of it
> Makes you mad enough
> Never to tire of it,
> Makes you hold all things tawdry and cheap for it;

If life seems empty and useless without it
And all that you scheme and you dream is about it,
If gladly you sweat for it,
Fret for it,
Plan for it,
Lose all your terror of God or of man for it;
If you'll simply go after the thing that you want
With all your capacity,
Strength, and sagacity,
Faith, hope and confidence, stern pertinacity;
If neither cold, poverty, famished and gaunt,
Nor sickness, nor pain
Of body or brain
Can turn you away from the thing that you want;
If dogged and grim you besiege and beset it
—You'll Get It—
(As quoted in the *Irish Missionary Handbook*, 1982.)

As a sophomore in high school I weighed 175 pounds. My brother David, a freshman, weighed a whopping 90 pounds. Only one year apart, yet I was twice his size. "How could you two be brothers?" everyone wondered.

But you see, David had a mountain of a spirit. And if a person could be a poem, David would be the poem I just quoted. Here is David's story in his own words:

I will never forget when I tried out for the freshman football team at Provo High. At five feet two inches and weighing only 90 pounds, I was even smaller than the stereotypical 98-pound weakling. I couldn't find any football equipment to fit me; it was all too big. I was issued the smallest helmet they had but still had to tape three ear pads together on each side of it to make it fit my head. The other players must have thought, "Hey, look at that mosquito with the balloon on its head."

I had to buy my own football pants because there weren't any small enough for me. My shoulder pads smothered me and my thigh and knee pads were wider than my legs. I must have been a pathetic sight.

I used to dread football practice, especially when we had to crack heads with the sophomores. And you must believe me when I say there were some sophomores who weighed over 200 pounds. We used to line up facing each other about ten yards apart with the freshmen on one side and the sophomores on the opposite side. When coach blew the whistle, you were supposed to hit your opponent until the whistle blew again.

I used to count the players in my line to see when my turn would come up, and then count the players in the sophomore line to see who would have the privilege of teaching me how to fly. It seemed that I always ended up getting the biggest, meanest sophomore as my opponent. "I'm dead meat," was my constant thought. I would line up against him, wait for the whistle, and in a moment find myself flying backwards and upwards through the air, wondering why I was playing this dumb sport. The next thing I knew I was lying on my back with an enormous headache. It was always hard to get up, especially when I knew that my turn would be up again . . . shortly.

That winter I tried out for the wrestling team. I weighed 93 pounds and wrestled in the 98-pound division. Even though I weighed in with all my clothes on after eating a big meal, I still couldn't tip the scales at 98 pounds. In fact I was the only guy on the team who didn't have to lose weight to wrestle. I wrestled to gain weight; I didn't particularly care for the sport. My brothers thought I would be a good wrestler because, unlike football, wrestling allowed me to compete with guys about my own weight. But to make a long story short, I was pretty bad. Some of my friends used to bet on how fast I would get pinned. "I'll bet Covey gets pinned in thirty seconds," they would say. And sure enough, I was down in thirty.

In the spring I went out for track. Maybe this would be my best sport. It turned out to be my worst. I tried every event from the mile to the hurdles, from sprinting events to relays. But as luck would have it, I was one of the slowest guys on the team, if not the very slowest. Little wonder—you should have seen my pencil legs. My knees were bigger around than my thighs.

I was only 14 years old at the time and obviously hadn't received the blessing of getting my height and weight early in my life, let alone the athletic ability I coveted.

One day after track workouts I just couldn't stand it anymore. "That's it," I said to myself. "I am sick, sick, sick of this." That night, in the privacy of my room, I set some goals I wanted to achieve during my athletic career at Provo High. I set both long-term and short-term goals. To be successful in my athletic pursuits, I knew I had to get bigger and stronger so I set goals in these areas first. I set long-term goals to be achieved by my senior year: to be six feet tall, to weigh 180 pounds, to bench-press 250 pounds. In football, I set a goal to be the starting wide receiver on the varsity football team. And in track I set a goal to be an all-state sprinter.

I wanted to be more than a starter, though. I wanted to be a leader, and I envisioned myself being captain on both the football team and the track team. A lot of nice dreams, wouldn't you say? At that moment, however, I was staring reality in the face. All 90 pounds of it.

I wasn't sure I could reach all these goals, but I was at least going to give it my all. I wanted to prove all my critics dead wrong. Then, when I achieved all my goals, when I showed them all I could make it happen, when I was bigger and stronger than they, they wouldn't mess no more with the Cov!

As I look back on my experience, I realize that it's not important to be big and strong or a great athlete. It is, however, important to always be striving to become better. It doesn't matter whether you want to be a great student or teacher, pianist or boy scout, dancer or doctor, or just an all-around great person. Be striving for something.

I knew the Lord would honor and respect my goals because my priorities weren't messed up. Spiritual things were always more important to me. Along with my Mr. Buff goals, I set goals to read the Book of Mormon and to memorize scriptures to prepare for my mission. These were my goals, this was my plan, and I was obsessed with it from my freshman until my senior year.

Let me illustrate. As part of my weight-gaining process, I made a rule that my stomach would never be empty. So I ate constantly. Breakfast, lunch, and dinner were merely three meals in an eight-meal day. I made a secret agreement with Cary Whittingham, the starting varsity linebacker for Provo High, who stood six feet three inches tall and weighed 235 pounds. He promised me that if I did his Algebra II homework, he would allow me to eat lunch with him every day for weight gain and for protection purposes.

I was determined to eat the same amount he ate, so each day at lunch I bought two lunches, three milks, and four rolls. We must have been a hilarious sight together! I was also taking my "Gain Weight Fast" protein powder along with my lunch. I would mix the sickening powder in each of my milks and nearly barf each time I drank it. The ingredients weren't the most thrilling: whole dried eggs, whey, desiccated liver, and so on.

During my sophomore year I began working out with my good friend Eddie Rowe, who was also yearning to get big. He added another requirement to my food list: ten full teaspoons of straight peanut butter and three glasses of milk each night before bed. All together, with this added requirement, I was eating about six thousand calories a day.

Eddie and I also set weekly goals regarding our weight gain. Each week we were required to gain two pounds. If we didn't "make weight" on the official weigh-in day, we were required to eat or drink water until we did. *No excuses accepted!*

I always dreaded the monthly fast Sunday. During Priesthood meeting, I occasionally slipped out with my friends to Winchell's doughnuts to feed my starving body. After all, I rationalized, going twenty-four hours without food could cause irreparable damage to my weight-gain program.

I did all sorts of crazy things to gain. My mom read an article that said if a young kid would sleep ten hours a night in a completely dark room and drink two to three extra glasses of milk a day, he could grow one to two inches more than he normally would. I believed this and followed it rigidly. After all, I needed to reach my goal of six feet and my dad's height of five feet ten inches wasn't going to help me. So I played Dracula. "Dad," I said, "I want the darkest room in the house." I got it. Then I put towels under the door crack and over the window. No light was going to shine on me!

Next I set a sleeping timetable as to when I would go to sleep and when I would wake up. I went to bed around 8:45 P.M. and got up around 7:15 A.M. This ensured me of 10½ hours of sleep. I adhered to this timetable religiously.

In addition, I drank nearly a gallon of milk a day. In the fridge I had my own milk carton with my name on it, "David's," which meant hands-off to everyone else. With my own carton, I didn't have to pour a glass but could drink straight from it, which made me look more tough and rugged—all part of the program.

On the workout and skill development side of things, I began lifting weights, running, and catching the football. Each day I would work out at least two hours. When Eddie and I lifted at BYU's weight room, we would check out the extra large shirts in hopes that one day we would fill them. At first I could only bench press 75 pounds, slightly more than the bar. It was kind of embarrassing.

But I was determined to get strong no matter what the cost.

Some days I felt like a lone man against the whole world. My family thought it was all fun and games. They, along with everyone else, didn't really understand my inner battle and the depth of my commitment. I felt that the Lord was the only one who really understood me or believed in me.

I got especially discouraged when I compared myself to friends who were twice my size. What really bugged me was that I was working five times as hard as they were, yet they were still bigger and stronger. Even worse than that, I had some friends, like Freddie Whittingham, who grew muscles while watching television. I swear it!

Comparing myself to others never left me with a good taste. Over time I learned that comparisons are plain stupid, because we're all on different timetables.

As the months passed I began to see results. Small results. Slow results. But results. By the time I was a sophomore I was five feet five inches and about 120 pounds. I had grown three inches and gained 30 pounds. And I was much stronger.

More important, I actually began enjoying the struggle I was undergoing. Some of my friends were naturally big and strong without any effort of their own, but because I had to work for it, because I had to fight for every pound, I was learning lessons and developing strengths they would never learn or develop.

One day, while reading a Louis L'Amour western, I came across a fight scene that illustrates this point. At that time, I identified wholeheartedly with the little guy, Matt Coburn, who takes on "Big" Thompson in a fist fight: "They circled each other warily. Matt was . . . sixty pounds lighter than Thompson. He had done his share of fighting and brawling, and he had learned long since that in most cases the very big man, having been large even as a boy, had never had to fight as much as a smaller man

had, and so had never developed the fighting skill or fe-
rocity a smaller man must need to develop to survive."
(*Empty Land* [New York: Bantam Books, 1969], p. 148.)

That was it exactly. I was Matt Coburn. I had to fight
to survive, and through the long hours of pain and sacrifice I would become tough and durable, even ferocious.
Moments like this inspired me.

Still, I constantly had to put up with negative comments from ignorant people. I especially hated it when
people would ask me, "How come you're so skinny? Why
don't you just eat more?" I felt like saying back: "You
idiot. You have no concept of the price I have been paying
to gain weight."

Once during my sophomore year, after I had gained ten
pounds over the past few months, the varsity football
coach asked me, "So, how much do you weigh now,
David?"

"About 120," I said proudly. I always said "about"
even though I knew exactly how much I weighed, even to
the ounce.

He snickered, "That's how much I weighed in sixth
grade."

After a while the negative comments no longer bothered
me; instead, they made me even more dogged, grim, and
determined to reach my goals.

By my junior year I was five feet eight inches and 145
pounds. I continued with my weight-gain program, the
running, the lifting, and the skill development. In my
track workouts, I made it a goal never to loaf, not even for
one sprint. And I never missed a practice, even on double
breakdown days. A double breakdown equals 4½ miles of
sprinting. You begin by sprinting 800 meters at your fastest speed, then 700, 600, 500, 400, 300, 200, 100. And
then back up the other way with a 100, 200, 300, 400, 500,
600, 700, and 800. It was a bear, but while many of the
other sprinters would skip out on double breakdown days,
I was there on the track giving each sprint my all.

Then suddenly the sacrifice and discipline really started paying dividends. I got real big, real fast. In fact I grew so fast that I have stretch marks across my chest. It looks as if I was mauled by a bear.

As I approached my senior year at Provo High I had reached my goal of becoming six feet tall and fell only five pounds short of my goal of 180 pounds. I became a starting wide receiver on the varsity football team, caught many passes, and scored several touchdowns. I was also selected by my teammates to be one of the four team captains.

My senior year in track was even more rewarding. Again I was selected as a team captain, and I became the fastest sprinter on the team, thus giving me the anchor leg on the 400-meter relay, which finished third in state. Also, because of my sub-50-second 400-meter time, I anchored the mile relay and ran third leg (400 meters) in the medley relay. Our medley relay finished second in state. I also qualified for state in the 100- and 400-meter races. In addition, I won the annual decathalon at Provo High. And to top it off, I was named all-state in track.

At the end of the year, weighing 180 pounds and bench pressing 255 pounds, I was awarded "Best Body" by the senior girls, the most coveted award of the year.

I did it! I really did it! I had now accomplished most of the goals I had set that night in my room years ago. I believe the Lord honored my goals and ultimately made it possible for me to achieve them. All along I felt his affirmation of me. Truly, as Napoleon Hill wrote, "Whatever the mind of man can conceive and believe, the hand of man can achieve."

As David told me his story, it became clear to me that he learned many significant lessons which are applicable to any "Big" Thompson we may face. I've named them "David's Two Best-Ever Insights."

Insight no. 1: *The process is more significant than the outcome.* Said another way, reaching for the stars is more important than getting there. It wasn't the titles of "team captain," "all-state," or "Best Body" that were important. It was the process that was important. By striving to become better and fighting an uphill battle, David developed inner qualities like discipline, diligence, mental toughness, and self-confidence. Even if he had fallen short of his goals despite all that effort, there would have been no loss; he still would have gained the qualities he did, which are much more lasting than an all-state or Best Body title.

Being a 90-pound punk may have been a blessing in disguise for David. It was his weakness, but it became his strength. I think everyone loves this scripture: "And if men come unto me I will show unto them their weakness. I give unto men weakness that they may be humble; and my grace is sufficient for all men that humble themselves before me; for if they humble themselves before me, and have faith in me, then will I make weak things become strong unto them." (Ether 12:27.)

This promise applies to weaknesses we can change. I also believe it applies to weaknesses we can't do much about, like the genetic endowments we're born with.

I remember reading something that Golda Meir, the late Israeli prime minister, said about herself. It was to the effect that at one point she recognized she was not a beauty and could not become so, but that in time this became unimportant to her, the work she had chosen having become much more significant in her life. Finally she perceived that, not having physical beauty to rely on, she had been compelled to call forth and develop inner strengths, and this actually gave her an advantage over women who depended on their good looks.

Think about it. Her weakness (lack of physical beauty) actually became her strength (forced her to develop her inner resources). People like Matt Coburn and Golda Meir, who may lack the natural physical or mental gifts of another, must fight just that much harder. And as my brother David discovered,

34

that struggle, that uphill battle, will produce qualities and strengths. That is how a weakness we can't do a lot about becomes a strength. When we recognize our weaknesses and are humbled by them, we are led to the source of strength, which is God.

So if you're not endowed with all the beauty, biceps, bucks, or brains that you covet—Congratulations! You just may have the better draw.

Insight no. 2: *You are of infinite worth, not to be compared with anyone else.*

Comparing ourselves to others makes us feel "like a wave of the sea driven with the wind and tossed" (James 1:6). We feel superior one minute and inferior the next. Comparing ourselves to others is like trying to compare apples and oranges; it just doesn't work. We're all much too different. And, as David learned, we all develop on different timetables, often not as fast as we would like. I love how Paul H. Dunn put it:

> I have noticed that daily we meet moments that steal our self-esteem. They are inevitable. Pick up any magazine; you see people who look healthier, skinnier, or better dressed than you are. Look around. There is always someone who seems smarter, another more self-assured, still another more talented. In fact, each day we are reminded that we lack certain talents, that we make mistakes, that we do not excel in all things. And amidst all this, it is easy to believe that we do not quite measure up in the great scheme of things, but are inferior in some secret way.
>
> If you base your self-esteem, your feeling of self-worth, on anything outside the quality of your heart, your mind, or your soul, you have based it on a very shaky footing. So you and I are not perfect in form or physical figure? So you and I are not the richest, the wisest, the wittiest? So what? ("On Feeling Inferior," Devotional Address at BYU, October 25, 1977, *BYU Speeches of the Year.*)

Being valiant in the testimony of Christ means that you not only believe in the unseen Christ but that you also believe in how he sees you. How does Christ see you? Everything he has done, his entire premortal, mortal, and postmortal existence, testifies to us that each of us is of infinite worth and has genuinely divine potential. Therefore, we cannot fully believe in Christ without also believing in ourselves. Someone once said, ''If you could envision the type of person which God intended you to be you would rise up and never be the same again.'' In other words, the key to releasing that ability inside of you is to believe that it's really there.

Ultimately, what we think of ourselves will largely determine what we become. This story told by Vaughn J. Featherstone beautifully illustrates this point.

Many years ago I heard the story of the son of King Louis XVI of France. King Louis had been taken from his throne and imprisoned. His young son, the prince, was taken by those who dethroned the king. They thought that inasmuch as the king's son was heir to the throne, if they could destroy him morally, he would never realize the great and grand destiny that life had bestowed upon him.

They took him to a community far away, and there they exposed the lad to every filthy and vile thing that life could offer. They exposed him to foods the richness of which would quickly make him a slave to appetite. They used vile language around him constantly. They exposed him to lewd and lusting women. They exposed him to dishonor and distrust. He was surrounded twenty-four hours a day by everything that could drag the soul of a man as low as one could slip. For over six months he had this treatment—but not once did the young lad buckle under pressure. Finally, after intensive temptation, they questioned him. Why had he not submitted himself to these things—why had he not partaken? These things would provide pleasure, satisfy his lusts, and were desirable;

they were all his. The boy said, "I cannot do what you ask for I was born to be a king." ("The King's Son," *New Era*, November 1975, p. 35.)

We were all born to be kings and queens, princes and princesses. We are all sons and daughters of God. If we believe this we will be able to do all that he commands, and resist all that he forbids. If we believe this we will discover gold and diamond mines of divine ability buried deep within us.

4

MISSIONS, DOMINOES, AND DIRTY LITTLE KIDS

*And now, if your joy will be great with one soul
that you have brought unto me into the kingdom
of my Father, how great will be your joy
if you should bring many souls unto me!*
—D&C 18:16

"And in closing, brothers and sisters, I must say that my mission was the best two years of my life." Elder Vernon smiled at the audience, gathered his papers, and sat down between his parents, who couldn't have been more proud.

A young man seated on the back row stared blankly ahead. "Not again. I can't believe he said that," he muttered to himself. "It seems every missionary says it was his best two years. Do they really mean it? What goes on out there anyway? I just don't know about this mission stuff. Is it really for me?"

At one time or another, every LDS young man asks these same questions. Along with other young people, you may get tired of hearing the often-repeated answer: "You must serve a mission." In addition, you may have a lot of personal fears and doubts about a mission, which you keep to yourself. And perhaps you feel that no one really understands you or your particular situation. You might say one of the following:

"I have a girlfriend I don't want to leave behind. I don't want to jeopardize our relationship. I mean, I really love her."

"I'm just not the missionary type. I can't memorize a thing. And I would hate to turn into one of those 'Holy Joes.' "

"Talking in front of people frightens me, especially people I don't even know."

"Why should I serve? I don't have much of a testimony. In fact, I've never even read the Book of Mormon."

"I have other plans right now. And besides, I can be a missionary in other ways."

"I doubt that I could ever live up to the expectations of my parents and be the kind of missionary my brother was."

"I don't feel worthy."

"I'm not worthy and the road back is just too long and too hard."

As for me, the thought of having to learn some strange and complicated foreign language made me shrink.

Such concerns are very legitimate and very real. And there is nothing wrong with having them. Most of us do. And why not? After all, serving a mission is not an easy task.

We've all heard many reasons why we should serve a mission. Some are better than others:

We have the truth.

We have been commanded to serve a mission.

A mission will strengthen our testimony.

A mission will build us a spiritual foundation for life.

Some reasons are not as good:

Everyone's doing it.

The "choicest" girls only marry returned missionaries.

The sons of Mosiah in the Book of Mormon served missions for still another reason: "Now they were desirous that salvation should be declared to every creature, for they could not bear that any human soul should perish; yea, even the very thoughts that any soul should endure endless torment did cause them to quake and tremble" (Mosiah 28:3).

But sometimes these reasons aren't sufficiently motivating for you and me, and don't seem to take into account our unique struggles. Sometimes we just need something more in order to break through the powerful why-not-to-serves. The key is to begin with the end in mind.

Each of us must realize that a mission may not be convenient. There may be a multitude of reasons for not serving. And a mission will require a sacrifice. But what else is new? Anything good in life requires sacrifice. It's been said that sacrificing simply means giving up something good (your plans, your time, your girlfriend, your doubts) for something better.

A runner, in the heat of the race and on the threshold of agony, is able to see the race to its end because through it all he can picture the finish line. The dieter, in the midst of potato chips and chocolate bars, is empowered to resist the cravings by seeing a thin body at the end of the tunnel. In like manner, the premissionary can face and overcome any doubt and any concern about serving if he can hold the end result firm in his mind's eye. That end result, that something better, is this: *If you will faithfully serve a mission you will influence the lives of hundreds of individuals forever.*

Even if you convert only one person, your influence for good will be far-reaching. I love a story told by Elder Harold B. Lee that illustrates this point.

I remember the story that Brother Charles A. Callis used to tell us. There was a missionary who went over to Ireland and had filled a mission of two or three years. They invited him to the stand to give his homecoming speech and he said to them something like this, "Brothers and sisters, I think my mission has been a failure. I have labored all my days as a missionary here and I have only baptised [sic] one dirty little Irish kid. That is all I baptised."

41

Years later this man came back, went up to his home somewhere in Montana, and Brother Callis, now a member of the Council of the Twelve, learned where he was living . . . and he went up to visit him. And he said to him, "Do you remember having served as a missionary over in Ireland? And do you remember having said that you thought your mission was a failure because you had only baptised one dirty little Irish kid?"

He said, "Yes."

Well, Brother Callis put out his hand and he said, "I would like to shake hands with you. My name is Charles A. Callis, of the Council of the Twelve of The Church of Jesus Christ of Latter-day Saints. I am that dirty little Irish kid that you baptised on your mission." (*Feet Shod with the Preparation of the Gospel of Peace*, Brigham Young University Speeches of the Year [Provo, 9 Nov. 1954], p. 1.)

As an Apostle, Charles A. Callis had a positive influence on thousands of people. Although the credit belongs to the Lord, think how pleased he is with that one missionary who was the catalyst for all that righteous influence.

In the Book of Mormon, Abinadi was commanded by the Lord to preach repentance to wicked King Noah and his priests and, as a result, was burned at the stake.

I can't imagine Abinadi's thoughts while at the stake, but I would think that he felt peaceful inside, despite any outside anxiety, because he had done exactly what the Lord had told him to do. At the same time, he might have felt disappointed, for perhaps he died believing that he had influenced no one, just as many missionaries come home believing that they had little success.

But the scriptures go on to say that there was one among the priests who believed the words of Abinadi and repented of his sins after the prophet's death. His name was Alma. And he became the next high priest, or prophet of the Church. Alma had a son known as Alma the Younger, who in his youth was disobedient but eventually came around, then became the next prophet. Alma the Younger had a son named Helaman who became the next prophet, who had a son named Helaman who became the next, who had a son named Nephi who became the next, who had a son named Nephi who became the next. This last Nephite was the prophet at the time Christ made his visit to the Nephites, almost two hundred years after the death of Abinadi.

In other words, six generations of prophets all came from the influence of one "missionary," Abinadi, who may have died believing that he had had little influence. Can you imagine how many people these six prophets directly or indirectly influenced? The numbers begin to be staggering.

To young men I have the chance to speak to, my personal message is: *Serve Missions.* Look beyond the reasons for not serving. Remember that even if you help to convert only a few people, or leave a few pamphlets at a few doors, that influence for good will spread over generations.

Young women, although you haven't been commanded to, you too can serve missions. And do you have any idea how much influence you have on young men? It is far more than you could ever imagine. Your support and enthusiasm for missionary work just might be the extra push a young man needs when he is at the crossroads of a mission decision. Some may disagree, but I also think that women have a greater capacity to love others. This is the key to missionary work. And that is why sisters can be such effective missionaries.

On my mission I had the opportunity to baptize an eighteen-year-old boy named Clive Reid. A wonderful convert. But wait. When Clive turned nineteen he decided to serve a mission and was called to London, England, where, by chance, my brother David was serving and got to train him. There Elder Reid became a mission leader and helped to convert many people. He returned to South Africa with a burning testimony and a desire to marry in the temple. He'll fulfill his Church callings and hopes to raise children in the Church who will grow up and go on missions also. Then the cycle begins all over again. Some might see only the baptism of one dirty little South African kid. I see the Lord working through me and then Clive and then count-less others to influence hundreds and eventually thousands of people.

It helps me if I think of it like this: Pretend you get called to serve your mission in Hawaii. Now, pretend you are fortunate enough to see twenty people baptized while serving there. Of those twenty people you baptize, five of them are young men, and three of those young men decide to serve missions. One goes to Colorado and converts thirty-five people, one goes to Scotland and converts fifteen, and another goes to Chile and converts one hundred fifty. Most of these converts will be nur-tured in the gospel, marry in the temple, and raise children in the Church. These children will later go on missions, convert people, marry in the temple, and on and on.

Serving a mission is like rolling a snowball down a hill and watching it grow. Or, it's like knocking over the first domino in an infinite chain of dominoes. And I believe that when we get to the other side people we've never met will come to us and say, "Thank you for baptizing my great grandparents. Because you faithfully served a mission, my family and I enjoyed the bless-ings of the gospel." The Lord said that if we bring just one per-son into his kingdom, our joy will be beyond compare (D&C 18:15–16). What about many?

Each of us is unlike anyone else. I love how Ruth Vaughn put it: "You are a once-in-a-lifetime, never-before-on-earth, never-to-be-again personality. Understand the importance of that." (James H. Fedor, comp., *The Pocket Companion of Inspira-tional Thought* [Bountiful, Utah: Mind Art Publishing, 1986], p. 45.) Think about it. Whether good or bad, we have been through experiences that no other person has undergone. And because we are all unique, with the help of the Lord we can reach and influence investigators that perhaps no other mission-ary could reach.

For example, while I was on my mission in South Africa there were times when, for one reason or another, I couldn't reach an investigator but my companion could. Why? Because he was different than me and could relate better to our investigator. Maybe the Fernandez family in Argentina will respond better to an aggressive personality. But the Matsuda family in Japan will respond better to a laid-back or quiet personality. Your uniqueness, whether loud, quiet, shy, or bold, may just be the spark leading to an investigator's conversion. Serving a mission may just be the most significant contribution you will ever make.

When I turned nineteen, I also had to make the mission decision. I had just completed a good season as the BYU junior varsity quarterback and, consequently, some felt that I shouldn't serve a full-time mission because I could be a missionary by being a good example as an athlete. Each case is different, but for me, in my situation, this didn't feel right. And since I had already made up my mind, as a young boy, that I was going to serve, there was really no decision to be made.

I sent in my papers and received my call. But before I opened the letter I went up into the mountains to be alone. This drove my family crazy. While up there I offered a silent and quick prayer: "Lord, before I open this letter, I want thee to know that I'm willing to go anywhere thou wouldst send me, except Idaho." (My wife's from Idaho.) Then I opened the letter and read, "You have been called to serve in the Johannesburg, South Africa, Mission."

"Wow!" I screeched. "South Africa! Where is it?"

It just so happened that the BYU football team won the national championship the first year I was away. In the opening game of that season, BYU played nationally ranked Pittsburgh on nationwide television. While my teammates were playing that important game, I was doing something even more important. I was baptizing a lovely, middle-aged woman, Ella Duarte, whose husband had just died. It was my very first baptism. And what a contrast! I'm sure my teammates were excited, but I wouldn't have traded that day for anything in the world. And I wouldn't have traded my mission for any other experience in the world, even a national championship.

Of the one hundred or so players on BYU's national championship team of 1984, fifty-two were returned missionaries. *Sports Illustrated* was so intrigued by this unusual "missionary team," that they decided to print an article on why BYU football players interrupt their careers to serve missions. They wanted to interview me in beautiful but turmoiled South Africa and three other football players who were currently serving missions: Scott Peterson in Bolivia, Don Busenbark in Brazil, and Duane Johnson in Kentucky.

On a Sunday in January of 1985, Gary Smith, the assigned *Sports Illustrated* reporter, arrived in Cape Town, South Africa. My companion and I picked him up at the airport and brought him to the mission home for an afternoon meal. He was unbiased, bearded, and looked like a granola mountain man. Incidentally, Elder Neal A. Maxwell of the Quorum of the Twelve Apostles was touring our mission at that time. I wondered if Gary realized what an honor it was for us to meet an Apostle and feel of his spirit. Gary spent quite some time quizzing Elder Maxwell and my mission president, Phillip Margetts, about our missionary system.

The next day we took Gary to a zone conference held with about fifty other missionaries. For around seven hours, Gary listened to emotional testimonies, motivational talks, and inspirational music. He sat in the back of the room totally bug-eyed and visibly moved. I imagine it was difficult for a nonmember such as Gary to fathom why so many young men and women would want to leave their homes, travel to an unknown land, pay their own way, and work relentlessly for eighteen or twenty-four months, all in the name of their beliefs.

On Gary's last day in South Africa, President Margetts said to me, "Elder Covey, take him tracting." So we made Gary put on a white shirt and a skinny tie and a-tracting we went. We taught many people that day, and Gary was able to observe the teaching process.

Later in the day we asked Gary if he would like to try some door approaches himself. He said he would. So we quickly taught him the standard approach. A young lady answered the door on his very first attempt, and Gary nervously said, "Hello, we're from The Church of Jesus Christ of Latter-day Saints. And we have a message we want to share with you. May we come in?"

"Do you have a church around here?" she asked him.

(We weren't going to help him.) He hesitated and said in a cocky manner, "Lady, we're branching out all over the world." She didn't let us in.

During the three days Gary was in our mission he participated in many discussions. He had the opportunity of talking with an Apostle, my mission president, many missionaries, and new converts. He received the Book of Mormon, other Church books, and numerous pamphlets on gospel principles. In short, we unloaded everything on him that we could in three days. He then left to interview the three other football-player missionaries.

Gary ended up writing a lengthy, fairly accurate, and positive article on Mormon missionary work—in a magazine that reached twenty million people. Many missionaries were thoughtful enough to write to me saying how that article helped them get into homes and teach. Gary later said, "That week we spent with Peterson in Bolivia turned our lives around." He and his wife, Sally, enjoyed Bolivia so much that they returned there to live for a year, while Gary taught English at an orphanage and Sally worked in the pediatric ward of a hospital. They even adopted a little Bolivian girl.

Although you will hear various opinions, you alone must decide whether to serve a mission. And it should be a private, careful, and prayerful decision. If you are at the crossroads of your mission experience, think on this.

While my dad served as a bishop on BYU campus, he had the following experience. There was a young man in his ward who was undergoing an immense internal struggle over whether or not to serve a mission. On one hand, because he was an active and faithful Church member and came from a family with a strong mission tradition, he felt he should serve. On the other hand, he was a serious and conscientious student. He strongly desired a medical career and felt that a mission might interrupt the strict academic curriculum required to achieve this end. He also felt that he could be a missionary through his medical service.

My father, as his bishop, held several counseling sessions with him, during which they compared and discussed the pros and cons of serving a mission. This young man was deeply torn and was struggling back and forth.

One day, as my father was walking down a stairway in the Jesse Knight building on BYU campus, he met this young man walking up the stairs. They had but a brief moment together. My father said to him, ''I've given a lot of thought to your situation and I just want to ask you one question: If you knew that by faithfully serving a mission you would influence hundreds of people, forever, would that influence your decision?'' He then left the young man to his own thoughts.

Many months later this young elder wrote to my father from his mission in Australia, reaffirming his feelings about that moment in the stairwell. He said that he couldn't get that question out of his head. It haunted him. All of his reasons not to serve were I-me-mine reasons. And the idea that he could influence hundreds of people forever totally eclipsed all of his legitimate but selfish considerations. There was no question as to what he should do. He related that he would never trade the experience he was now having as a missionary for any other experience in the world.

You can serve a mission and still accomplish everything else you desire. Lots of my friends have. Look at the 1989-90 starting BYU basketball team. Kevin Santiago, Marty Haws, Andy Toolson, and Steve Schreiner were all returned missionaries. And the other starter, Mark Durrant, interrupted a promising career to serve a mission.

In a Priesthood session of general conference, BYU head football coach LaVell Edwards had this to say about athletes and missions: ''Will going on a full-time mission have an adverse effect on a future athletic career? . . . It has been our experience that if a young man decides to go on a mission, he cannot only play well when he returns, he will often play better." ("Prepare for a Mission," *Ensign*, November 1984, p. 44.)

If you will make the sacrifice to serve, things will take care of themselves. Your family will be blessed. Your girlfriend will be fine. Your athletic or academic ability won't abandon you. You can develop a testimony. You can master the language and the discussions. You can become worthy.

But you can't afford to pass up this opportunity. More important than any reason not to serve is the fact that out there somewhere—maybe in Mexico, or Alaska, or Tonga, or even Idaho—there's a family, a young man, a young woman, or even a dirty little kid waiting to hear Christ's message through unique you. Make a commitment right now that you will be there to proclaim it. And then we'll all watch the dominoes begin to fall.

5

MY WORST
BIRTHDAY EVER

If you can meet with Triumph and Disaster
And treat those two impostors just the same;
. . . .
Yours is the Earth and everything that's in it,
And—which is more—you'll be a man, my son.
—Rudyard Kipling

"What was the high point and the low point of your career?" the young female reporter flippantly asked. Immediately, dozens of images flashed across my mind, bringing with them both happy and painful memories.

"The high point of my career," I blurted out, "was beating Air Force in my very first start. And my low point . . ." I wasn't about to share with her my deepest feelings. It was none of her business.

"My low point," I continued, as she hurriedly scribbled on her pad, "was waking up after reconstructive knee surgery and realizing I had months of rehabilitation ahead of me."

That's what I told her. But, to be honest, I had encountered much lower points than that. Take, for instance, my birthday the year before.

I'll never forget that beautiful autumn day. A few trees on the top of Y mountain were beginning to turn red, the morning air was getting chilly, and my greatest fear in life was to be twenty-five, bald, and unmarried. Luckily, though my hair was thinning, I was only turning twenty-four, and I was married to the best woman ever.

I drove to the stadium, two hours before kick off. A few players were already milling around in the cold locker room when I arrived. I sat down at my booth, glancing at my helmet and jersey hanging in front of me.

As part of my pregame dressing routine, I neatly slid three pieces of Wrigley's spearmint gum into my sock. Every player has his own superstition when it comes to games. Some guys swear that if they wear a certain pair of socks, or a certain undershirt, victory is ensured. You wouldn't think that by the smell, but they believe it. My superstition was gum. I guess I was convinced that chomping on gum made me feel more confident, or at least made me look that way.

I picked up the game program and there I was on the front cover—a full-size action shot. What a present! "Wouldn't you know it?" I thought. "Here it is my birthday and I'm on the cover. This is definitely going to be my best birthday ever."

BYU was hosting the UTEP Miners. A year earlier we had beaten the Miners on their home turf in El Paso, Texas, in a remarkable comeback victory. So this year the Miners wanted what I wasn't going to let them get: revenge. This day was our day. I could feel it in the air. Clear sky. Warm day. And a stadium decked with thousands of fans dressed in blue and white, munching down mustard hot dogs, listening to Paul James's pregame spectacular, and waiting to turn loose their personal, weekly, frustration buildups.

On our first possession, we garnered four consecutive first downs on back-to-back plays. Our offense was smelling of confidence as we scored, to take a 10-0 lead.

"Red Right Slot," I barked out in the huddle, "Switch Zing . . . 62. Z-Corner . . . On One . . . On One . . . Readyyyyy . . . Break." I swaggered up behind the center, the vibrant "break" still ringing in my head. Our star receiver, Chuck Cutler, was put in to run the "Z-Corner" route, meaning that Coach Chow, who called the plays up in the press box, wanted pay dirt. And we all knew this play would get it. Since the creation of BYU's passing offense, we have scored a million touchdowns on "62-Z-Corner." Funny that our opponents can never seem to stop it.

The snap came, I dropped back, and sure enough there was Chuck in the corner of the end zone, three yards ahead of his defender. I cocked and threw. As the ball slid off my fingertips I thought, "Dang, I underthrew it." But wouldn't you know it. It was caught for a touchdown! A blowout was in the making. I was having a birthday to remember.

Here it was only the first half, and I had thrown for nearly three hundred yards. It seemed to be one of those I-can-do-no-wrong days.

Then something strange happened. Perhaps the previous week's late-night study sessions had combined with long practices to produce some fatigue, for I was finding it difficult to concentrate. Before the half ended I threw two interceptions, which led to UTEP scores. Our defense folded, and, although we had convincingly outplayed the Miners, we trailed going in at the half.

"Our whole season depends upon this second half," Chuck Cutler roared, as he stomped into our locker room. He was right. This was a crisis. Since we had already lost one WAC game, losing this one would knock us out of the WAC race, a depressing prospect considering it was only the third game of the year.

I sat down on a stool and tried to collect my thoughts.

"Sean," said one of the coaches. "Come in here for a minute." I apprehensively trailed him into the coaches' strategy room.

"Listen closely. We're going to give you one more drive in the third quarter, and if you don't produce, you're out. Understand?"

"Yes, coach," I muttered.

Somehow, this didn't exactly motivate me. But I guess a coach must do what he feels is best.

The half-time rest was all I needed to renew myself, for in the third quarter my concentration was back. The team's wasn't, however, and our offense sputtered on two consecutive possessions, allowing UTEP to maintain the lead.

I nervously paced the sidelines, wondering if they were really serious about this benching stuff. Then I saw Coach Edwards.

"Sean," said coach, "we're going to give the other guy a chance for a few series, to see if he can spark things. We may put you back in depending on how things go. So stay ready."

I said nothing, but inside I argued, "No way. This can't happen to me. It's not right." I felt sick. I felt embarrassed. I didn't know how to react. In my nine years of playing competitive football I'd never been benched before, no, not even for a play. And now this. It was my birthday.

A thousand emotions passed through me as I stood helplessly on the sidelines and watched Ty Detmer lead the team to victory in the waning moments of the game. I was excited by the victory but sickened at having been benched.

In the raucous locker room after the game, my quarterback coach pulled me aside. "This is going to be the hardest thing you'll ever face. So just grit your teeth and bear it. You're still our starter." What he meant was that having to face everyone—fans, friends, and reporters—after being benched, would be a miserable experience. And was he right!

A big birthday party with family, relatives, and friends was planned for me at my house after the game. It was the last place I wanted to be, but I went anyway.

I opened the door and everyone gave me that we-don't-know-what-to-say look. "Happy Birthday, Sean! Wasn't that a great victory?"

"Sure was," I whimpered. The only people I wanted to speak with were my wife Rebecca and my dad. They alone understood how I was feeling inside.

I felt awkward during the whole party, especially when a friend of a friend, whom I hardly knew, said to me basically, "Hey, tough going out there today. Bummer of a birthday." I wanted to smash his face in. This was definitely my worst birthday ever.

Two weeks later we played Utah State University in a Friday night contest at Cougar Stadium. This time the outcome was far different. I threw for 360 yards, two touchdowns, and no interceptions as we slaughtered the Aggies 37–6. It was the best performance of my career to that point. I felt marvelous.

Little did I know that two weeks later I would outdo that performance, raising many eyebrows and throwing for 490 yards against the Horned Frogs of Texas Christian.

One week after my 490-yard production, I found myself in the hospital, undergoing orthoscopic surgery, after tearing some cartilage in my knee. I would be out of action for at least a week. My knee was never the same from this point on.

Only two weeks after surgery I played again and led our team to a high-scoring victory over Air Force, ensuring us a bowl bid.

One week later, the University of Utah pommeled us in a big upset. My knee felt terribly unstable on Utah's artificial turf. I was again benched in the third quarter.

I felt up one week, down the next. The media praised me one game, cursed me the next. I was healthy one day, injured the next. My season, as Charles Dickens put it, "was the best of times, it was the worst of times. . . . It was the season of Light, it was the season of Darkness."

I was riding an emotional roller coaster, up and down, high and low. But that is the nature of football. That is the nature of life. Going into a game you never can tell what might happen, which way the ball will bounce. You may thrash your opponent and be a hero. Or you may get thrashed and be a goat. Then again, you may blow out your knee. Who can tell? That is the crazy thing about football. That is the crazy thing about life. The only thing you have complete control over is your response to what happens to you. And that is what counts!

Understanding that life, by its very nature, is seasonal or cyclical is my first of three keys to remaining unruffled through life's highs and lows. I say highs because handling success with all its praises and honors can be an even greater challenge than handling defeat. My father once heard Harold B. Lee set apart a stake president. In the blessing, Elder Lee advised this man that each time he achieved a significant success, he should go into his private closet and give all the credit to the Lord. Good advice for any of us.

On the other hand, when we experience downers or setbacks, you and I have the tendency to think that something is wrong with us, that we are weak, and that successful people never feel this way. Nothing could be further from the truth. Who hasn't been down in the dumps and struggled in one way or another? Who doesn't fight his own internal battles? Some just hide it better than the rest of us.

It is so easy for us to murmur and become bitter. To feel that our setbacks, our problems, and our knee injuries are unwarranted, unfair, undeserved. "This isn't right," we complain. "Here I am, working hard, striving to live a good life, and yet things aren't going as planned."

But deep down, I think, we know better. Living the gospel doesn't promise us a life free of backache or heartache, or a life full of popularity and prosperity. It does, however, promise us the ability to successfully manage our highs and lows and to find shelter under the eaves of gospel perspective while the storms rage outside.

After my roller coaster season ended, the doctors advised surgery again in order to diagnose and repair my unstable and weakening right knee. I brooded while going under the anesthetic, anticipating the worst. Hours later, I woke to learn that my anterior cruciate ligament, the main stabilizer in the knee, had severed and disintegrated. I'd played without it the last four games of the season. This was a surprise to both the doctors, to the coaches, and to me. With a reconstructed knee and months of rehabilitation before me, I realized that my chances of maintaining the starting position come next fall would be slim, at best.

Over the next few months, the hospital rehab center became my home. The leg machines became my best friends. Daily, I spent many hours in hard and monotonous rehabilitation. I also tried to reconcile the triumphs and traumas of the past season. I recalled the words of Lehi to his son, which my stake president, Douglas Smoot, had shared with my fiancée and me just before our marriage. "Jacob . . . thou hast suffered afflictions and much sorrow. . . . Nevertheless, . . . thou knowest the greatness of God; and he shall consecrate thine afflictions for thy gain." (2 Nephi 2:1-2.)

How powerfully this passage struck me! Think of it. With the Lord's hand, you can actually turn any setback into a triumph, any stumbling block into a stepping-stone. This hope-filled idea is my second key to remaining steady through my highs and lows. Maybe this is what the Lord meant when he said to a suffering Joseph Smith, "All these things shall give thee experience, and shall be for thy good" (D&C 122:7). Or it may have been what the philosopher Gilran was thinking about when he wrote: "That self-same well from which our laughter rises was often times filled with our tears. The deeper that sorrow carries into our being, the more joy we can contain."

I have often wondered why it is that so many valiant people have had such rough lives? Was it just coincidence that Spencer W. Kimball and other modern prophets had physical problems, some of them near-death experiences? Was it just coincidental that Joseph was sold into Egypt as a slave by his older brothers, and was later unjustly imprisoned? Why did our Savior need to descend below all things? It seems God does his best renovations on us when we are our humblest. Truly, "Man's extremity is God's opportunity."

Remembering that our downers are usually "but a small moment" (D&C 121:7), that these "too shall pass," and that another great performance lies just around the corner, is a great source of comfort to me. Moreover, there is often an unseen purpose behind each of our despairing moments. "Sweet are the uses of adversity," said Shakespeare. But this is hard doctrine to swallow. It reminds me of a tough experience my older sister

57

Cynthia went through in high school. High school seems to be especially full of highs and lows. My mother recorded Cynthia's story in the *Ensign:*

> Being elected cheerleader of her high school seemed to be the most important need in [Cynthia's] life. She had worked for several months, practicing every day doing cartwheels, flips, splits, and cheers, till we were all relieved when the final cuts came. There were tears every time one of her close friends was eliminated and hope surged as she progressed to the final election assembly. "Oh, Mother, I'm praying so hard to win. The Lord says you can ask for any righteous desire of your heart and this is mine." It seemed a reasonable request to us, too. She was firm and solid in the Church and socially popular. . . . We thought she would be a good influence for the Church.
>
> At the final assembly tryouts things went beautifully. She was in great form, her cheer was original, she was well known and received as much or more applause than anyone else. She seemed a cinch to be one of the five winners.
>
> She was absolutely crushed when she lost. It was only by a few votes, but she lost.
>
> "Mother, you just don't know how important this was to me," she sobbed. "It's one of my lifetime goals. Why did the Lord let me down when I prayed so fervently? It wasn't just for myself. I was going to use this office as a good, solid influence for the Church. I study the scriptures every single night. I do missionary work constantly. I stand up for the Church in every situation; I work my head off in the ward and on the stake youth council and then one time I ask for help—what do I get? It isn't as if I didn't do my part. I practiced for six months. I couldn't have tried harder."
>
> I was a little disillusioned myself. So good. So faithful. So deserving. I didn't have too many answers, but I told

her there must be a good reason and through prayer and study she would come to understand why.

The very next month she was asked to be one of the high school seminary officers. . . . They said they really needed our daughter's creativity and missionary talents to draw people, and this year was a crucial one for gaining a positive stronghold.

That year she had many profound spiritual experiences. She developed deep, meaningful friendships and was a positive influence in helping several people come into Church activity.

Later she told me that she gradually came to an understanding of herself through fervent prayer and study of the scriptures. "I wanted to be cheerleader more than anything else, but the Lord knew I needed this other experience more. I needed more spiritual growth. It was a hard experience, but I know in my heart it was right." (Sandra Covey, "Teaching Our Children to Pray," *Ensign*, January 1976, p. 63.)

Near the end of my roller coaster season, I went to the private study booths found in the basement of the humanities building at BYU. I sat down on a hard chair and pulled out my American literature textbook, enjoying the visual privacy the booth provided. I soon became aware of two guys who were talking away in the adjacent booth. Their conversation was of no interest to me, that is until I became the main topic. I don't recall their exact words; I do, however, remember that one guy was my worst critic, the other my best defender.

"I don't think Covey should play. They should have pulled him long ago," said the one.

"I don't agree at all," returned the other. "Covey is much more experienced than Detmer and it will show in the tough games."

"No way. Did you see him last game? I thought Detmer did much better."

"Yeah, but he was playing against the second string defense."

After a few minutes of this, I had had just about enough. So I stood up tall, squared my shoulders, and entered their booth. My critic, shocked upon recognizing me, turned bright red. He was a little guy. By his shaking I could tell he thought I would pop him one. It was quite enjoyable.

"Listen," I rebuked, "if you're clueless about what's happening on the field, you have no right to say anything." That was all I said. The situation itself had beaten him up sufficiently.

Fans often take athletics far more seriously than players do. On another occasion, a die-hard Cougar Club member spoke to my wife so offensively about my playing that she was brought to tears. Events such as these occur often in our lives. And they often hurt—deep down. People and relationships, just like events, may also be seasonal and fickle. An experience I had with my younger sister illustrates this point:

Late one afternoon, there came a knock at the door.

"Who could that be?"

Again the knock—much louder now.

"All right already. I'm coming." I opened the door and there stood my younger sister, heaving and sobbing uncontrollably.

"What's wrong?" I asked, leading her in, although I knew exactly what was wrong. This was the third uncontrollable-sob-on-the-doorstep that month.

"He is so rude," she sniveled, wiping her red, swollen eyes. "I can't believe he did that to me. It was so mean."

"What did he do this time?" I asked. I had heard some pretty good ones and couldn't wait to see if this one was any better.

"Well. You know. He asked me to come over to his house to study and all," she whimpered between snivels. "And, while we were studying, some other girls came to visit him. And he acted like he didn't even know me, in front of them."

"I wouldn't worry about it," I said wisely. "I used to do that kind of thing all the time when I was young and dumb."

"I know. But I've been dating him for two years," she blubbered. "And worst of all, he even told them that I was his sister."

"That's a pretty good one," I thought. To me it was funny. To her it was real and painful. But I wasn't worried about my sister. Since her life wasn't centered on her boyfriend, this common episode wouldn't throw her. I figured that after the initial shock, she'd flow through it steadily.

Sure enough, two days later she was on cloud nine over the same guy.

This brings me to my third and most important key to remaining steady through my highs and lows: Build your foundation upon Christ and his gospel, because everything else—relationships, health, circumstances, events—can be fickle, volatile, unpredictable, and unstable.

On the other hand, building our foundation upon Christ makes us, as Elder Neal A. Maxwell writes, "grounded, rooted, established, and settled."

My experience has been that building our foundation upon any source other than Christ is like building upon a cheese puff. These alternate foundations are full of air. They won't stand the heat.

Guy was his high school's star basketball player. After years of high-fives and continual praise, he began to derive his sense of self-worth from his basketball prowess. "I'm cool because I run rings around everyone on the court," he thought. While in practice one day, a freak accident ended his career. The applause suddenly stopped. His identity was so shaken that he spent the next two years of his life wandering about, trying to find himself again.

Jennifer was in love! She had just entered her second year of college and had also discovered the boy of her dreams. Over the next several months Jennifer centered her emotional life around her boyfriend and his promise that everything would work out between them. She was devastated when he left her for someone else. A year passed before she could even bring herself to trust another boy or to date again.

For Karen, being popular and having many friends became the most important thing in her life. She made sure she wore the right clothes and only hung out with the "in" people. But the time came when she had to make a decision between being "with it" and keeping her standards. The thought of being rejected by the popular group so frightened her that she abandoned her standards and lost her self-respect and reputation in the process.

All these everyday people would have remained steady in their trials had they built their lives upon a rock and not a cheese puff. Those who are founded upon Christ and his gospel can take risks and can leap outside their comfort zones. They remain unruffled through the storms of life because they carry their own weather inside them. They can afford to be vulnerable because they have an unchanging core, a "foundation whereon if men build they cannot fall" (Helaman 5:12). Adversity may shake them temporarily. But it cannot uproot them.

So how do we build our foundation upon Christ and his gospel? Plenty has already been written about that. For now, I like the way my dad says it: "If you will spend twenty minutes a day with the Savior of this world, you will spend eternity in his presence." Try it for thirty days. Then judge it. I find that if I will spend at least twenty sincere minutes each day in prayer and scripture study, I can cope with any setback, rise above any hurt, and even flow steadily through any bad birthday.

6

ME A
QUARTERBACK?

> *You see things as they are and*
> *say, Why? I dream of things that*
> *never were and say, Why not?*
> *—George Bernard Shaw*

I stepped timidly into Coach Drury's office. How would I tell him?

"So, what do you think about it, Covey?"

"Well, I did what you told me. I went home and thought about it. I decided that if you want me to play quarterback, I'll do it. But I really want to be a running back, because that's what I'm good at, running."

"I see," he returned. "But we think Sean Covey is a quarterback, and that's what we want you to play. Okay?" He glared at me with his I-know-what-I'm-doing eyes. I had no choice. Coaches have a way of giving you your opinion.

It was my freshman year at Provo High. During the first day of tryouts for the freshman football team, the coaches decided that I would be their quarterback. It was by default. Nobody else could throw. The only reason why I could throw was that my older brother Stephen, being a varsity receiver, made me throw him hundreds of passes every day. But I never wanted to be a quarterback. I dreamed of being a running back. Quarterbacking was much too complicated and, besides, I'd never played it before.

I remember that first Saturday morning as we boarded the yellow school bus to travel to Springville to play their freshman team. I hated those bus rides before games. The ride is always real quiet because coaches don't appreciate the players talking before games. It's all part of the football tradition. They feel that if you talk, your mind's not on the game. Something like that. I was always too high-strung to talk, anyway. I felt as if I was going off to war, never to return.

But once the game started, that fear always seemed to leave. And by the end of the game, football was the greatest thing ever invented, or so I felt, until the next game and the next bus ride came around. You know, one of those love-hate relationships.

The Springville game was my first start as a quarterback. It showed. As we boarded the bus in defeat, I remember brushing back tears. I felt happy and discouraged at the same time. Discouraged because I had thrown three interceptions and wondered if I'd lost the game for us. Happy because the game was over, the pressure was off, and the weekend awaited.

From this shabby beginning, little did I imagine in my wildest dreams that I would eventually have the opportunity to quarterback for BYU, the premier passing school in the nation. The habit of goal setting made all the difference. This single habit has influenced my life more than any other habit, hands down. My experience as a senior at Provo High School is an illustration.

At the start of my senior year, our varsity football team met all together at Uncle Bud's Park in Oak Hills. It was a little park across the street from my house, where, each day after school, I'd play my favorite childhood game—inter-neighborhood, anything-goes, tackle-football skirmishes. We'd planned this meeting a few days before. No coaches or trainers were invited. Just a bunch of sixteen- and seventeen-year-old boys. The season was only days away so the spinal goose bumps were beginning already. It seemed kind of corny and all, but we'd come together in order to set some team goals.

The legislation began. Everyone started pitching in their two bits. "Let's win all our games except one." "Let's win our region." "Let's kill 'em." Finally someone blurted, "I say we set a goal to take the state championship." This got everyone's attention very quickly. "State championship? Are you serious?" we all thought. Provo High had never, in its history, won a state championship in football. In basketball, yes, many times. But never in football. Yet the more we thought about it, the more achievable it became. Besides, we were all too proud for any one of us to admit it was beyond our reach.

We didn't write this goal down, but we did do the equivalent. We copied an inspirational quote onto three-by-five index cards, giving one to each team member. It represented our goal. It read:

> There is no chance, no fate, no destiny,
> that can circumvent, hinder, or control,
> the firm resolve of a determined soul.

There is something about a team that is united in a common goal. It is a feeling, a sense of confidence, an almost tangible desire. We had it. For the second straight year, we captured the region crown and headed into the state play-offs with reckless abandon.

The previous year our state championship dreams had ended in tragic fashion. We were battling the Jordan Beetdiggers in the quarterfinals of the single-elimination, state play-offs. The game came down to one play. We trailed 28–23. Eleven yards to go. Five seconds on the clock.

Taking the snap, I faded back to pass . . . four . . . I spotted my receiver, my good friend Larry, wide open in the end zone . . . three . . . I cocked and threw . . . two . . . the ball landed right in his hands. Our team, and our coaches, and our fans were ready to freak out in victory—and then, to our horror, he dropped it! The buzzer then sounded to end the game and our season.

We hadn't spoken to Larry since.

This year was going to be different. We got off to a fantastic start in the state tournament by slaughtering our first two opponents. Now we were one of only four teams remaining. Again we had to face the Beetdiggers of Jordan.

Unlike the year before, this game wasn't exactly a thriller. Before we could even tie our shoes, Jordan jumped to a 17–0 lead. We were shocked. "Well, at least we came this far," I thought, doubting that we could ever stage a comeback. At the half, we staggered into the locker room physically beaten and emotionally shaken by the far hungrier Beetdiggers.

The locker room was cold and damp. It was filled with decaying lockers, grimy benches, and a few disregarded folding chairs. Coach Henderson's halftime chew-out session was nothing to look forward to either. But I must admit, he was in marvelous form. According to coach, Fine Unga (pronounced Fee-Knee), our Tongan fullback and noseguard, was the only one who had any guts. "I'll leave you to yourselves to think about it," coach concluded. I always hated it when coaches said things like that. My conscience and pride always got to me worse than anything the coaches could have said.

Coach then exited, and silence followed. But Fine had been praised too much to just sit there. We all knew that. He was now obligated to say something. My brother David recalls looking over at Fine. "He looked like a mad dog," said David. "He had red hot fire coming out of his eyeballs, he was so angry."

See, Fine, like most other Tongans I've known, was one tough player. Once he told me that if I wanted a washboard stomach like his, I should eat rotten food and garbage. Somehow, I think he meant it.

Wham! Wham! Wham! Fine broke that dreadful silence by smashing in a few lockers with his helmet. Flying chairs came next. Then, in his own form of English, and with a few words I won't repeat, he snarled: "Man, guys! We're getting our butts kicked. C'mon! We gotta beat these guys. They're a bunch o' wimps. We gotta come out fired up!" That is what he said. But I heard something else. "There is no chance, no fate, no destiny, that can circumvent, hinder, or control, the firm resolve of a determined soul."

As you watch a high school game from the stands, munching a hot dog and chatting with friends, you are led to think, "Isn't this fun, Ethel. All those kids out there having just a grand time. Nothing like a little healthy competition." But to the players it's far different. My mom has a sign hanging in her kitchen that captures the football player's mentality. It says: "Football isn't a matter of life or death. It's much more important." When you want to win real bad, and your head's ringing, and your body's aching, and coaches are screaming, and you've sacrificed thousands of hours to get where you are, the game goes far beyond important. For a high school boy, it's war.

Fine was a literal animal in the second half. A one-man show. A needed spark. When it would have been easy for us to fold and surrender, all our preparation—the hours of running stairs, throwing, and lifting weights together, the well-developed friendships, the comradery, and yes, the love—all came to our aid. We clinched that game in the final minutes. It came down to this: We were too accustomed to winning, too uncomfortable with losing. And, five months earlier, we had set a goal.

The following week, we beat the Vikings of Pleasant Grove in the state championship game. Ironically, Larry, who had dropped the pass the year before, snagged a crucial forty-yard bomb to preserve our victory. Our goal was now complete. Provo High School's first ever (and we hope only ever) football state championship! We did it! We really did it! Oh, and by the way, we began speaking to Larry again.

This state championship experience taught me all about the power of goal setting. It can make all the difference in our lives. "Without the pursuit of goals," wrote Lowell L. Bennion, "life is drab, quite meaningless, confusing, and might even be idiotic." (Paul H. Dunn, *The Ten Most Wanted Men* [Salt Lake City: Bookcraft, 1967], p. 180.) Yet, sometimes, when we hear the word *goals*, we cringe. It guilt trips us. It reminds us of all the goals we should be setting and achieving. Besides, there is so much written about it, who knows where to begin? I agree. But, with your permission, I thought I'd add to the confusion by slipping in my four principles of highly effective goal setting.

Principle no. 1: Count the Cost

Let's pretend you set a goal to read the scriptures at least twenty minutes each day over the next two months. Good and fine. But now, before you begin, count the cost. Think it through. What will it require? What must you sacrifice? For instance, at times the mattress will be more inviting than Moroni. You will be busy. Papers and reports will be pressing. You won't feel like it. A dozen reasons for not reading will arise. Finding time to read might mean giving up enjoyable late nights with Johnny Carson, or treasured moments with *Popular Mechanics*. Now, having counted the cost, ask yourself: Am I willing to make the sacrifice? Do the benefits of scripture study outweigh the cost? If not, then make the goal more bite-size. Section off bites you are willing to sacrifice for. Maybe you should set a goal to read for a one-week period instead of a two-month period. Then, next week, take another bite. Slowly, your personal power and self-trust will increase.

Self-trust is like a bank account. Each time you make a promise to yourself and keep it, you make a deposit. Each time you make a promise to yourself and break it, you make a withdrawal. Nothing will rob us of our self-trust and self-confidence faster than making and breaking promises to ourselves.

For example, have you ever had the experience of setting your alarm clock to get up bright and early, only to hit the snooze button thirteen times? When I have, I feel like a loser for the rest of the day. For me, it often becomes the first in a long series of personal defeats. The Lord puts it this way: "For which of you, intending to build a tower, sitteth not down first, and counteth the cost, whether he have sufficient to finish it? Lest haply, after he hath laid the foundation, and is not able to finish it, all that behold it begin to mock him, saying, This man began to build, and was not able to finish." (Luke 14:28–30.)

On the other hand, I believe that the fastest way to gain control of our lives and to increase our self-trust is to make a promise to ourselves and then keep the promise. Make a promise; keep it. Line upon line, precept upon precept, bite after bite. Each time you set a goal or draw a plan, make it a habit to first count the cost. What will it cost to improve my relationship with my wife? What will it cost to lose this extra weight? What will it cost to learn to play the piano? If it costs too much, break it down into smaller, achievable pieces. Remember, the Lord taught that "out of small things proceedeth that which is great" (D&C 64:33).

Principle no. 2: Write Down Your Goals

It's been said, "A goal not written is only a wish." There are no ifs and buts about it; a written goal carries ten times the power. About this important point, that is all that needs to be said. Write them down!

Principle no. 3: Do It!

I read a story once about Cortés and his expedition to Mexico. With over five hundred men and eleven ships, Cortés sailed from Cuba to the coast of Yucatán in the year 1519. On the mainland he did something no other expedition leader had thought of: he burned his ships. By cutting off all means of retreat, Cortés committed his entire force and himself to the cause. It was conquest or bust.

"To every thing there is a season," says the Preacher (Ecclesiastes 3:1). A time to say, "I'll try," and a time to say, "I will." A time to make excuses, and a time to burn your ships. Don't procrastinate. Don't find excuses. Just do it, taught President Spencer W. Kimball. Of course, there are times when try-ing is all we can do. But I also believe there are many, many tasks and goals that, if we firmly commit ourselves, we can ac-complish. The capacity is within us. Would you lend two thou-sand dollars to a business partner who said, "I'll try to return it"? Would you enter into the marriage if, when asked to take you as lawfully wedded husband or wife, your partner said, "I'll try"?

Get my point?

Once we are fully committed to doing a task, our power to complete it will increase. "If you do the thing," said Emerson, "you will have the power." Each time I have committed myself to a goal, I seem to dig up gold mines of willpower, skill, and creativity I never thought I possessed. Those who are committed always find a way to win.

I have been unable to locate a source for the following quota-tion attributed to W. H. Murray. I quote it here because it com-municates what happens to us when we make a commitment and say, "I will."

> Until one is committed, there is hesitancy, the chance to draw back, always ineffectiveness. There is one elemen-tary truth, the ignorance of which kills countless ideas and splendid plans, that the moment one definitely commits oneself then providence moves too. All sorts of things begin to occur which would never otherwise have oc-curred, and a whole stream of events issues from the de-cision, raising in one's favor all manner of unforseen inci-dents and material assistance which no man could have dreamt would have come his way. I have learned a deep respect for one of Goethe's couplets:
> Whatever you can do or dream you can begin it.
> Boldness has genius, power, and magic in it.

The fourth principle of highly effective goal setting is found in the next chapter under the title "The Spiritual Creation." I have given it a chapter of its own because I believe it's the most powerful but least understood principle of all.

"There are two worlds," said Leigh Hunt. "The world that we measure with line and rule, and the world that we feel with our hearts and imagination" (James H. Fedor, comp., *The Pocket Companion of Inspirational Thought* [Bountiful, Utah: Mind Art Publishing, 1986], p. 17). The next chapter is all about this imaginative world of ours.

7

THE SPIRITUAL
CREATION

*Though it be long, the work is complete
and finished in my mind . . . and it rarely
differs on paper from what it was in my imagination.*
—Mozart

"All things are created twice. First, spiritually; second, physically," said Dad. It was another one of his hyper-creative family home evening lessons. Together with my parents and all seven of my brothers and sisters (Joshua, the youngest, wasn't born yet), I was standing on the roof of a tall building overlooking the construction site of the new Salt Lake City ZCMI Center. Somehow, Dad had also managed to bring along his newfound friend, the chief contractor, who happened to be overseeing all the construction.

"What's all this spirit stuff?" I asked, brushing a strand of blond hair away from my face and gazing birdlike at my surroundings.

"When the Lord created the earth," Dad continued, "he first drew up the plans in his mind, or created it spiritually, before the mountains, the seas, the animals, or anything was ever created physically."

"What ya talkin' 'bout, Dad?" my little sister cut in.

"You see that huge building being constructed." He pointed. We all looked in awe. Across the way was a massive edifice two football fields wide and several stories high built of steel and iron. "This is the framework of the new ZCMI Center. And our friend here is going to take us into his special room, where we can see this entire structure in blueprint. You see, kids, the ZCMI Center has already been created."

Filled with curiosity, all ten of us followed Dad's mysterious friend into a room stuffed from floor to ceiling with bundles and bundles of blueprints.

Dad's friend pulled out and ruffled through a large stack. "See here," he said, spreading out a huge sheet across the table. "The plans for the electrical systems for the entire ZCMI Center are shown in this stack. There are also stacks of blueprints that show the heating, air conditioning, and plumbing systems, even down to the last drain."

"Wow, that's quite a lot of paper!" we all thought.

"It's quite amazing, isn't it, kids?" grinned Dad, thrilled with himself for planning this awesome family home evening adventure on the rooftop. "Yes, kids, every floor, every door, every drinking fountain, even the tiniest detail is created in blueprint before a nail is ever hammered into place," he continued, stroking his shiny bald head.

"In the same way, children, all of us should draw up blueprints for our lives." Dad's voice now took on that serious tone it always did when he got into his teaching mode. "We can create our own futures and plan our own destinies in our mind's eye."

"But why is it important to draw up blueprints, Dad?" asked my little brother David. "Why can't they just start building?"

"David, without blueprints, the builders wouldn't know where to begin or what they're trying to accomplish. There would be confusion and chaos. By accident, they might easily build an unstable foundation, which wouldn't hold up. Even worse, without a blueprint to refer to, they could end up with an entirely different building than the one they had originally intended. It is the same with people."

I gave Dad my blank stare. It meant, "Keep explaining."

"Sometimes," Dad continued, "because people fail to plan, they wander through life, never quite sure what they stand for or what they want to accomplish. It's like running a race in three different lanes. Lacking direction, they often build their lives upon unstable foundations. Eventually, under the weight of temptation, pressure, or discouragement, these foundations will collapse. But the worst case of all is the person who ends up with an entirely different life than the one he had intended. He was so busy building that he forgot what he was building. This is like reaching the top rung of the ladder, only to discover that it's leaning against the wrong wall."

"Now, that makes sense," I smiled.

It was now many years later in another family home evening lesson. Dad was again teaching us kids about the spiritual creation.

"Dad, how do we draw up blueprints in our head?" I flopped down onto our cozy, rust-colored couch. My brothers and sisters were sprawled out in various positions across the living room floor.

"It's simple, Sean. You just have to use your imagination. I believe that the Savior himself extensively used this creative gift during his ministry. The scriptures record that Jesus often retired to the mountains to pray alone. During these prayers, I believe he walked through his entire ministry with his Father, step by step, before he ever did it in public."

"But, Dad, on a practical scale, how can we do what he did?"

"Let's try it. I want you all to close your eyes and relax. Breathe deeply. Clear your mind of all worry and concern." I was looking around to see if everyone was going to take him seriously.

"Now, in your mind's eye, imagine the day ahead of you. What are your plans? What are your challenges?

"Put yourself into a challenging situation. See yourself at school, huddled with your friends in the hallway. Make it as realistic and detailed as possible. You're having a wonderful talk-it-over session when suddenly the group begins bad-mouthing the new kid on the block. See yourself resisting the urge to join in. Instead, you defend that person, even though it goes against the grain. Your friends are all surprised. In your heart, feel the satisfaction of knowing you did the right thing.

"Now, imagine another scene. Let's suppose you have a bad temper, which often offends and hurts other people. Pretend your younger sister borrowed your favorite blouse without asking, and then left it lying wrinkled on the floor. You feel anger welling up inside you. You're ready to spout off at the mouth. Now, see yourself restraining those instincts, holding back your anger. Picture yourself being calm. With gentleness you explain to your sister why you want her to ask before she takes something of yours. Now, feel the warmth inside. Feel the satisfaction you get from being your own master."

"Hey, this is fun," I giggled, imagining myself giving the Heisman trophy acceptance speech.

"Yes it is, Sean. And also very effective. If we are facing a big challenge or a tough moment, such as playing in the championship game or speaking at church, we can rehearse outstanding performances in our heads beforehand. We can picture ourselves keeping our commitments, overcoming temptations, and being the people we would like to be. Then, when the real battles approach, it's as though we have already conquered them. We have visual blueprints of our performances already imprinted in our minds. I suggest that every morning, in our daily prayers, we develop the habit of walking through and creating our day with the Lord."

Dad's voice echoed through the living room. Little did he know how much use I would make of these spiritual creation lessons later in my life.

It was the night before my first start for BYU. Tomorrow afternoon, at jam-packed Cougar Stadium, we would battle the Air Force Academy football team on national television. As mentioned in chapter one, Air Force, at the time, was nationally ranked and boasted the best defensive tackle in the nation. I lay on my bed, staring at the ceiling. If I played well this game I could solidify myself as the starter. If not, it might be not only my first start but also my last start. After eight years of preparation, to think that my fate lay in the outcome of sixty minutes seemed the ultimate injustice.

After practice, each night that week, I'd spent a few minutes rehearsing the upcoming game in my mind. Tonight I would do it one more time.

I spread out my arms and legs, sank into my feathered comforter, closed my eyes, and began to breathe deeply. To relax myself further, I imagined lying on a plot of grass near the banks of a gentle brook in the mountains.

I then saw tomorrow's game. There was Cougar Stadium filled with blue and white fans, Mount Timpanogos jutting up in the background. I heard the roar of the crowd, smelt the crisp autumn air, and felt the green grass firm beneath my cleats. In my mind's eye, I rehearsed each one of our plays. I saw those linebackers eyeing me as they fell back into coverage. Air Force is blitzing. It's third and long. What should I do? It's man coverage. We expected zone. What should I do? This play won't work. I must get out of it. What should I do? Again and again I pictured myself doing all the right things, making all the right reads, and throwing completions and steaming bullets for touchdowns.

I imagined myself performing in each tough situation that could arise. I executed in rain and snow, ignored raving coaches, escaped blitzing linebackers, gripped wet and waterlogged footballs. I even envisioned come-from-behind victories. Nothing could throw me. If opposition struck—an interception, a body-breaking hit, a lost opportunity—I would give my wristband a flick, signifying flicking away and forgetting the past.

It was a good thing I had done this, for the next day, after one quarter of play, our offense had garnered a grand total of minus six yards, while Air Force led momentously 10–0. I had flicked my wristband nearly threadbare. The coaches were ready to pull me. The crowd was ready to boo.

But I'd already seen this movie the night before. In fact, I'd starred in it. Thus, I was able to remain calm and collected and to come through for the team. In the end, we upset Air Force 24–13.

The spiritual creation is just one of many names for this imaginative power of ours. It is also called self-visualization, envisioning your goals, imagining your best self, daydreaming, or whatever. We all use it much more than we are aware of, in both constructive and negative ways. For example, visualize your past mistakes or failures and see how it makes you feel. Too often we allow these visual memories to hold our futures hostage. On the other hand, in color and in vivid detail visualize your greatest success. Now, feel those juices flow.

When we are caught in life's quagmire, our imaginations can transport us to far-off and better places. In practice, I'd often get fed up with all the hollering and yammering. To help me escape, I wrote this poem:

> When passes thrown fall at receivers' feet,
> And coaches raise their voices to a shriek,
> Upon the mountaintops my vision falls,
> And in my mind I throw some awesome balls.

For me, setting goals and writing them down is not enough. To achieve them I must first see them. I believe we haven't even begun to tap the constructive uses of our imaginations, not just in athletics but also in daily living. I hesitate to share the following personal experience but do so in hopes that it will better illustrate the power and practicality of the spiritual creation in our everyday lives.

We all seem to have idiosyncrasies. For me, I need time to emotionally adjust to big decisions. Maybe it extends back to my childhood. For instance, my parents tell me that when I was a young boy they would need to tell me weeks in advance before they left on a trip. Otherwise it was hard for me to emotionally adjust to their being away. An announcement one day before they left made me unsettled.

During the winter of my sophomore year at BYU, I fell in love with a girl named Becky Thatcher, as in *Tom Sawyer*. Our relationship progressed much faster than I could ever have imagined, leading to our setting a marriage date only seven months after we began dating. Our wedding day would be just one week before the football season began. For me, this was fast. But deep inside I felt confirmed and settled about who I was marrying and the timing of the wedding.

At this time in my life I also felt an incredible amount of pressure. As well as from school, I felt pressure from rehabilitating a badly torn knee ligament, carrying the weight of being the BYU quarterback, and speaking continually at firesides and youth conferences. And now I was getting married, forever. All this seemed too much for a psyche that preferred ample time to sit on, think about, and adjust to major decisions. And marriage is as major as they come. Knowing what we as Latter-day Saints know about marriage, it is a wonder we ever do it.

Consequently I found it hard to relax in my life and felt very anxious much of the time. This seems funny to me now, but at the time it was a real concern. Bringing myself around to getting married forever seemed like the biggest hurdle I had ever faced.

I needed to do something about my anxious state of mind. And putting off the wedding date wasn't the answer. Instead, I decided that if I could imagine myself being married, just as I had imagined myself performing in games, perhaps that would help me relax and adjust to the big day ahead.

I drove to the parking lot within the Provo Temple grounds and found a shaded area beneath a tree, where I could be alone.

Lying down in the grass, I closed my eyes and let my imagination go to work. I envisioned my wedding day in the Salt Lake Temple in vivid detail. I pictured the room in which the wedding would be held. I saw Rebecca's family, as well as my family and close friends, gather around the marriage altar. I felt myself kneel down and look across the altar at Rebecca, as we listened to the beautiful words of the ceremony.

As I imagined this, it seemed as if parts of me were fighting against my getting married. It is difficult to describe in words just how I felt. But it seemed nearly impossible for me to see myself go through the entire ceremony. My mind would get stuck, or I would lose concentration, and I had to try again and again. At last, after much mental exertion, I was able to see it to the end.

I had visualized the ceremony so vividly and in so much detail that I felt as if I had actually gone through it. I felt very peaceful and very sober. Like a tiny chick enclosed within a hard shell, I was trying to break out of a comfortable and familiar environment. And in a sense, by seeing myself go through with the marriage, I made the first crack in my hard shell. And having seen one crack, I then knew that I could make others and could eventually break out entirely.

There is nothing psychic, mystic, or strange about this imaginative quality of ours. It is not the medicine of quacks or the wonder drug of gurus. And it is not just for athletes.

"So just what is it?" you may ask.

It is powerful.

It is uniquely human.

It is creating your future in your head.

It is seeing yourself with "an eye of faith" (Ether 12:19).

It is writing down your private constitution or drawing up your personal blueprint.

It is dealing with your struggles in private before arriving in the high-pressured public arenas.

I love Thoreau's words, "Explore your higher latitudes . . . be a Columbus to whole new continents and worlds within you."

I firmly agree. I believe we are governed far too much by our past, far too little by our imaginations. No matter what your past has been, your future is an unwritten biography.

Go ahead. Create it!

8

FROM STARTER
TO BACKUP

*To laugh often and much; to win the respect of intelligent
people and the affection of children; . . . to appreciate beauty;
to find the best in others; to leave the world a bit better,
whether by a healthy child, a garden patch, or a redeemed
social condition; to know even one life has breathed easier
because you have lived. This is to have succeeded.*
—Ralph Waldo Emerson

I will never forget the hoopla after we beat Air Force in my
very first start for BYU. ESPN must have gotten sick of my
mother calling in, because they named me "Player of the
Game." In the locker room, after the game, I was mobbed by reporters sticking microphones and television cameras in front of
my sweaty face. "Sean, how does it feel to win your first game
as a starter?" "Will you be BYU's next all-American quarterback?" "Tell us what happened on that first long bomb you
completed." It seemed like everybody wanted to talk to me. I
couldn't believe it. "Life doesn't get any better than this," I
kept saying.

My mom must have been on the phone all night, because the
next day the newspapers all said wonderful things about me. I
was congratulated at church. I was congratulated at school. In
fact, people who I never even thought were my friends phoned
to say, "Way to play, dude."

The next week I led our team to a high-scoring victory over
San Diego State. And wouldn't you know it. The backslapping

increased. It seemed I could ask for and receive favors from almost anyone. The letters started pouring in. I was flattered by all the attention. It all made me feel important. It all made me feel great.

As I have already related, I underwent reconstructive knee surgery at the end of that year. I also had to miss spring practice. During the winter, spring, and summer, I worked my tail off trying to get my knee ready for fall camp. When fall camp came around, although my knee hadn't fully recovered, I surprised everyone. I was playing pretty well. But a couple of weeks before the season opener, Coach Edwards called me into his office and told me that I wouldn't be the starter. Ty Detmer was playing outstanding football.

I felt sick. This didn't seem right. I had worked too hard to secure the starting quarterback job to lose it now. I also wanted to use the position for good purposes, to help young people. My goal of becoming an all-American quarterback was washing down the drain. The previous two years I'd been throwing touchdown passes. Besides, I was a senior and my replacement was only a sophomore.

We played New Mexico in the opening game of the season. I sat on the bench most of the game. At the end of the game I was put in just to hand the ball off and to run the clock out. I felt as humiliated and embarrassed as I had once felt excited.

In the locker room after the game we all knelt as Coach Edwards offered our traditional post-game prayer. After the prayer, the reporters invaded the locker room. By now, I knew them all personally. They had interviewed me so many times in previous years. But this time they weren't crowding around sticking microphones in my face. They simply walked by me and said, "Hello, Sean, it's good to see you," as they walked away to interview Ty. I learned quickly that reporters aren't interested in interviewing backups. This happened every single game for the rest of the year. I no longer enjoyed being in locker rooms after games. There were no more phone calls to congratulate me. It was as if everyone had forgotten that I had ever played for BYU. Suddenly, I didn't feel so important. Suddenly, I didn't feel so great.

As a backup I had to make a decision. I could badmouth and become bitter or I could make the most of the situation. Luckily for me, I'd seen people in situations such as mine—in athletics and in life—who had become bitter. I'd seen people who had hung on to grudges for years. And once that poison was in them, it seemed to fester and infect. It simply isn't worth it, even if it seems justified.

I thought about Joseph of Old Testament times, who at the young age of seventeen was sold into Egypt as a slave by his older brothers. Later, in Egypt, despite being a faithful servant in the household of Potiphar, he was falsely accused and imprisoned, where he remained until he was thirty. But like the prophet Job he never became bitter, he never badmouthed or bickered. He made the most of each situation and eventually became second only to Pharaoh. After being given the very sourest of lemons, Joseph truly made lemonade.

For me, lemonade sounded better than poison. I was no longer the starting quarterback, but I could be successful in other ways. Rather than complaining, I began supporting Ty and the rest of the team. I worked hard and prepared myself for each and every game as if I were the starter. I maintained a positive attitude. And do you know what? Most of the pain left me. In many ways, I felt a greater sense of contribution as a backup that year than I did as a starter the year before. Had any reporters cared to ask, I would have had to say that, personally, it was a very rewarding year.

Going from starter to backup was no picnic, and it's not usually the success story anyone would write or read. But it was a success story for me because it brought home a principle I have always believed in. There are two types of greatness: true or primary greatness, and secondary greatness. Secondary greatness is throwing a touchdown pass, wearing the nicest clothes, having the most things, or being the most popular. These give us the applause of the world. Almost everything we are exposed to, such as radio, television, and magazines, teaches us that wealth, beauty, awards, fame, and possessions are what make a person great. Then when we lack Porsches or popularity, when we aren't the starter, we seem to feel insignificant and unimportant. This is a big lie. These things have value but not a lasting value. They are only secondary.

Primary greatness comes from our character—what we are inside. Primary greatness means having quality relationships with God, our family, and our friends—even if it's only one friend. Primary greatness is being honest when it's tough to do so, being kind to someone who is unpopular, sticking up for your beliefs when it's not cool. Primary greatness means caring more about what God thinks of us than what the crowd thinks of us. These things have lasting value.

You've already read about the Olympic track star, Eric Liddell, who wouldn't run on the Sabbath because it would go against his own internal standards. Eric is one of my heroes, because he had the courage to put primary greatness (his beliefs) ahead of secondary greatness (his running ability), even if it meant giving up his ultimate dream.

My football experience taught me again what I had learned so many times before, that if we derive our feelings of self-worth from any other source than the quality of our hearts and our true identity as eternal children of God, we are building upon shaky ground. We should never feel we are better than another because we have achieved some form of secondary greatness ("I'm better than he is because I'm a better athlete, or I drive a nicer car"). And we should never feel we are less important than another because we haven't achieved some form of secondary greatness ("She's better than I am because she's a student officer, on the honor roll, or more popular"). Comparisons only rob us of our self-esteem. After all, in one way or another, aren't we all backups?

Instead, let's derive our self-worth from things that really matter. I love a story told by Spencer W. Kimball. After President Kimball had sealed a couple in the Salt Lake Temple, he was approached by a happy father:

"Brother Kimball, my wife and I are common people and have never been successful, but we *are* immensely proud of our family. . . . This is the last of our eight children to come into this holy house for temple marriage. They, with their companions, are here to participate in the marriage of this, the youngest. This is our supremely happy day, with all of our eight children married properly. They are faithful to the Lord in church service, and the older ones are already rearing families in righteousness."

"Success?" I said, as I grasped his hand. "That is the greatest success story I have heard. You might have accumulated millions in stocks and bonds, bank accounts, lands, industries, and still be quite a failure. You are fulfilling the purpose for which you were sent into this world by keeping your own lives righteous, bearing and rearing this great posterity, and training them in faith and works. Why, my dear folks, you are eminently successful. God bless you." (*Faith Precedes the Miracle* [Salt Lake City: Deseret Book, 1972], p. 260–61.)

I, like you, have dreams of greatness. I know of people who seek after primary greatness, who are big of heart and true of character. These are my heroes. I've also seen many achieve secondary greatness at the expense of primary greatness. This is a tragedy. It is like climbing the mountain of success and, upon triumphantly reaching the top, discovering that you've climbed the wrong mountain altogether.

Let's you and me seek for primary greatness, first and foremost, and then, as Jacob says, if we "obtain riches" or any form of secondary greatness, we will do so "with the intent to do good," to serve our fellowmen (Jacob 2:19). There may not be any reporters crowding around the servants. But remember, the Lord taught that the servant is the greatest of all.

EPILOGUE

Football isn't important. The lessons I learn from it are. That is why I love sports so much—because of the precious insights you can draw from these microcosms of life.

I'll never forget when we played the University of Utah in my sophomore year. This was the big affair of the season, of course, and I was determined to have a whopper of a game.

That week was brimful of television and newspapers, radios and reporters, hype, parties, paraphernalia, and all that other stuff which accompanies big-time college football and an in-state rivalry. It is a way of life for us.

At kick off that stadium was rocking. All sixty-five thousand fans drenched in blue, white, and red. Everybody was at the game waiting to cheer their hearts out for their team. You could feel the excitement between your fingers.

The game was a literal dogfight. Downright tough. By the third quarter, when neither team could pull ahead, the tension was cranked up a notch.

"C'mon now. We need a first down," I barked out as we broke the huddle. Taking the snap from center I sprinted to my right, waiting for my receiver to break open while a bent-on-destruction U of U linebacker closed in swiftly. Running up-field, he met me running downfield, just under the chin, and his massive frame firmly slammed all 180 pounds of me into the green.

Things went black.

Next thing I knew, I was on my back, being wheeled down a corridor of the hospital, comprehending what had happened.

My sister Catherine was shaking my feet, crying, "Can you feel them?"

"Of course I can feel them. Now, leave 'em alone."

The attendant asked me if I wanted to watch the remaining minutes of the game on TV. For some reason I didn't care to.

My family and some friends visited me faithfully in the hospital that evening, along with a few players and coaches. It was a long, long night. All alone, I had much time to think.

What contrast! Here was I, at the center of the big event. The passion! The pride! The excitement! The importance! And like a game, it all ended, it all changed—just like that.

How grateful I am for my friends, my family, my beliefs, and my God!

How much I love that foundation which is unchanging!

ABOUT THE AUTHOR

Sean Covey was born in Belfast, Northern Ireland—while his father was mission president there—and was raised in Provo, Utah. He graduated from Provo High School, where he led the football team to its first state championship and received Utah's 3-A division Most Valuable Player award for football.

Sean served a full-time mission to Cape Town, South Africa, and speaks Afrikaans. He attended Brigham Young University, where he earned the starting quarterback position on the varsity football team. He led the team to two postseason bowl games; was twice selected ESPN Player of the Game; was voted Honorable Mention All-WAC by the media; and earned academic all-conference honors for three consecutive years. He graduated with a degree in English, earning Brigham Young University's highest graduation distinction, University Honors. He was awarded the 1990 Kimball Award by the BYU Cougar Club, given for athletic and academic accomplishment.

Sean enjoys all sports, especially snowskiing, waterskiing, motorcycling, and snowmobiling. He is a popular motivational speaker to youth and adults at academic, athletic, religious, and civic conferences and workshops. *Fourth Down and Life to Go* is his first book.

The author is married to Rebecca Thatcher Covey, and they are the parents of one son. Sean is presently doing management consulting in Boston, Massachusetts.